GUILT
by
ACCUSATION

Also by Alan Dershowitz

GUILT

by

ACCUSATION

The Challenge of Proving Innocence in the Age of

#MeToo

ALAN DERSHOWITZ

HOT BOOKS

Hot Books may be purchased in bulk at special discounts for sales promotion, corporate gifts, fund-raising, or educational purposes. Special editions can also be created to specifications. For details, contact the Special Sales Department, Skyhorse Publishing, 307 West 36th Street, 11th Floor, New York, NY 10018 or info@skyhorsepublishing.com.

Hot Books® and Skyhorse Publishing® are registered trademarks of Skyhorse Publishing, Inc.®, a Delaware corporation.

Visit our website at www.hotbookspress.com.

10 9 8 7 6 5 4 3 2 1

Library of Congress Cataloging-in-Publication Data is available on file.

ISBN: 978-1-5107-7780-4

Cover design by Brian Peterson

Printed in the United States of America

Table of Contents

ACKNOWLEDGMENTS

This book could not have been published so quickly without the help of my wife, my children, and my friends. Special thanks to Aaron Voloj, Hannah Dodson, Nicholas Maisel, and Maura Kelley, as well as Alan Rothfeld and Ken Sweder.

Dedicated to my loving wife, Carolyn Cohen,
who guides me, advises me, and supports me.

A Note to Readers

The #MeToo movement has generally been a force for good, but as with many good movements, it is being exploited by some bad people for personal profit. Supporters of the #MeToo movement must not allow false accusers to hurt real victims by hiding behind its virtuous shield, turning it into an exploitative sword against innocent people.

For more information and updates, please see www.skyhorsepublishing .com/9781510757530/guilt-by-accusation/

Introduction

I magine how it would feel if you—or your husband, father or son—were falsely accused of a heinous sex crime by a woman you never met.

Imagine further how you would feel if you had conclusive evidence—in the accuser's own words—that she never had sex with you.

Now imagine that you also had recorded evidence—from her lawyer's own mouth—that it was "impossible" for you to have been in the places she claimed to have had sex with you and that she was "simply wrong" in accusing you.

Imagine even further that you discovered that your false accuser had a sordid history of falsely accusing other prominent men for money, and that she was falsely accusing you because she felt "pressured" by her lawyers who promised her a big payday.

Finally, imagine that despite this evidence, many people continued to believe the false accusation, just because "women who are abused don't lie."

That is the situation I and my family have been facing over the past five years. Although I am the victim here—the victim of a deliberate frame-up motivated by money—I am being treated as a perpetrator, despite the fact that I have done absolutely nothing wrong. My reputation has been trashed, my family has suffered, my retirement has been ruined, my health has been affected—all because a woman with a long history of lying decided, at the urging of her lawyers, to perjuriously include me without a scintilla of evidence in a list of men to whom she says she was trafficked by the notorious Jeffrey Epstein, whom I had represented a decade earlier.

After reading this book and seeing the indisputable evidence of my innocence and the total lack of evidence that I ever met my false accuser, no reasonable, open-minded reader will be left with any doubt. But at this stage, before seeing the evidence, I'm asking readers simply to assume, for purposes of an emotional and intellectual experience, that I am totally innocent, and to imagine how you would feel if you or a loved one were being subjected to what I have been put through over the last half decade. If this can happen to me—a man who has the resources to fight back—it can happen to anyone.

In order to understand—and feel—how this false accusation has upended my life, the reader must be put in my position prior to the accusation being made. I was a 76-year-old retired law professor (I'm now 81) with a controversial professional history. I had represented some of the most despised criminal defendants of our time, many of whom were guilty, but some of whom were innocent. Half of my clients were poor and could not afford to pay legal fees, so I represented them pro bono. These included many women, some of whom were victims of sexual, physical and psychological assaults. Some of my female clients are well-known, like Mia Farrow, Patricia Hearst, Leona Helmsley, Sandy Murphy, Sylvia Zalmonson and Maryam Rajavi; some are not, like the woman whose husband locked her up in a mental hospital, the wife who killed her abusive husband, the Harvard student who was sexually harassed by her professor and the mother who was denied custody of her 8-year-old daughter because she had left her husband for another woman. Other clients included death row inmates and victims of human rights abuses. I also represented filmmakers, actors, writers and publishers whose controversial works were censored.[1]

Although some of my clients had been falsely accused of serious

1   For a description of my cases and career, see *The Best Defense* (1982), *Chutzpah* (1991) and *Taking the Stand* (2013).

crimes, including murder, they all had preexisting relationships with their alleged victims. Moreover, the evidence was often ambiguous. There were grey areas, and doubts that had to be resolved under the law in their favor. I had never had a black-and-white case in which the accused had not even met the accuser. So despite my long experience in representing both the innocent and the guilty, I had never been involved in a case like this one. In all other #MeToo cases, the accused and the accuser had known each other: they had been intimate or had worked together. The issues were consent or harassment, which are often grey areas. Mine was the first in which there was no evidence that the accused and accuser had even met. It was "a zero-sum game," but it wasn't a game. Either I was absolutely guilty of a heinous crime, or my accuser was absolutely guilty of perjury for making up an entirely false story. There was no middle ground.

I had taught about totally false accusations involving crimes ranging from espionage to murder: Alfred Dreyfus; Menachem Mendel Beilis; Leo Frank; the "Scottsboro Boys" and others.[2] I had felt vicariously what it must be like to be subjected to a Kafkaesque labyrinth of lies. But I had never personally experienced it. Nor did I ever expect to, despite the controversial nature of my public persona and career.

In addition to representing controversial and unpopular clients, I had written hundreds of provocative articles and dozens of controversial books about hot-button issues, such as terrorism, torture, affirmative action, preventive detention, Israel, Iran and sexual assault. Of my forty books, eight had been best sellers, including *The New York Times* number one best seller, *Chutzpah*. I had taught thousands of students and lectured and appeared on TV before millions of audience members and viewers. My public image was confrontational and adversarial.

As the *Boston Globe* once put it: "If Dershowitz isn't getting in your face about something, it's as if he's not doing his job."[3] Very few people were neutral about me: I had fans and detractors. People either loved or hated my provocative views and the ways in which I expressed them.

---

2   See, Albert S. Lindemann, *The Jew Accused: Three Anti-Semitic Affairs Dreyfus, Beilis, Frank, 1894-1915* (1992). I write about the Leo Frank and Scottsboro trials in "America on Trial" (2004), pp. 218-226; 276-282

3   Alex Beam, Alan Dershowitz Takes the Stand, *Boston Globe*, Oct. 3, 2013.

Professionally, I was among the most controversial professors and lawyers in America. And I relished that status. I enjoyed being at the center of controversy for my ideas, principles and legal activities.

I was at the apex of my career, being honored for my life's work by awards, honorary doctorates and efforts to create a professorial chair in my name at Harvard. Presidents Clinton and Obama wrote letters of praise when I retired from Harvard, and when I turned 75, Obama wished me "Many more years of advocacy, mischief and great fun." The reference to "mischief" was about my iconoclastic and controversial political views.

There was nothing controversial or mischievous about my private life, and certainly none about my sexual activities. At the time of the accusation against me, I had been married to my wonderful wife Carolyn for nearly 30 years. My first marriage ended in divorce, and I raised my two sons. I met Carolyn seven years after the divorce. We have a great marriage and a wonderful daughter.

I am very different in my personal life than in my professional life. With family and friends, I avoid conflict. Family members consider me a pushover. I rarely argue and when I do, almost never win. I do enough arguing in court and on TV. When I come home, I want peace and quiet rather than conflict. The same is true among my close friends, who don't recognize what my son Elon calls "the Dersh TV character." I once complained to the late actor Ron Silver, who played me in the film *Reversal of Fortune*, that he had done a great job portraying me as a lawyer, but he had not captured the real me as a family man. He replied: "I'm playing the public Alan Dershowitz—the one people see on TV and in the newspapers. I can't get to know the private Alan Dershowitz well enough to play him, and frankly the public isn't interested in that side of you." (I only wish that were still true.)[4]

In my Harvard classroom, I was also tough and confrontational—though with a smile—because my job was to prepare law students for a confrontational career in a highly adversarial legal system. But

4   Alan M. Dershowitz, Reversal of Image: Watching Someone Playing Yourself, *New York Times*, Oct. 14, 1990.

outside of class, I was supportive and agreeable, as my students and mentees will confirm.

In my fifty-year teaching career at Harvard, I had many female research assistants, secretaries, students and colleagues. My wife and I invited my students to our home every year. Not a single complaint had ever been lodged against me for sexual (or any other) misconduct. My students, assistants and friends all know that I don't flirt with, hug or touch anyone other than my wife. That's not who I am. I am also a cautious person in my personal life, and I would never have risked destroying my hard-earned reputation or personal integrity by doing what I was accused of.

So when I was accused at the end of 2014 of having sex on seven occasions with an underage female who I had never met, no one who knew me and Carolyn believed the accusation, even when it was circulated around the world. People who didn't know me—who knew only the "Dersh TV character"—had no reason to disbelieve the accusation, because they were unaware of the long history of false accusations made by Virginia Roberts Giuffre, of my unblemished history at Harvard, and of the evidence proving my innocence. But that accusation was leveled before the advent of the "#MeToo" movement, and many of those who read about the accusation were then prepared to apply a presumption of innocence or at least of skepticism.

When I categorically denied the accusation in the media and swore in court that I had never even met or heard of my accuser, many in the general public believed me, especially because my accuser refused to repeat her accusation to the media. She made it only behind the so-called "litigation privilege," which protects false accusations made in court filings from defamation suits.[5] They also believed me because I produced all my travel and other records during the period Giuffre knew Epstein, which proved I couldn't have been

---

5   As Judge Jose Cabranes recently put it, "Our legal process is already susceptible to abuse. Unscrupulous litigants can weaponize the discovery process to humiliate and embarrass their adversaries. Shielded by the 'litigation privilege,' bad actors can defame opponents in court pleadings or depositions without fear of lawsuit and liability. Unfortunately, the presumption of public access to court documents has the potential to exacerbate these harms to privacy and reputation by ensuring that damaging material irrevocably enters the public record." Brown v. Maxwell, No. 18-2868 (2d Cir. 2019).

in the exotic places—including Epstein's Caribbean island and New Mexico ranch—where she falsely claimed to have had sex with me. Any doubts about the accuracy of these records was resolved when the former Director of the FBI reviewed them and concluded that "the totality of evidence found during the investigation refutes the allegation made against Professor Dershowitz." Even Giuffre's own lawyer, after reviewing my documents, concluded that it would have been "impossible" for me to have been on the island and ranch during the relevant time period, and that his client was "wrong . . . simply wrong" in accusing me. She must have confused me with someone else, he surmised.[6]

Then it turned out that Giuffre had been paid $160,000 by the *Daily Mail* to accuse several men, including President Bill Clinton, Vice President Al Gore and his then-wife Tipper of having been entertained by Epstein on his notorious island. She provided the *Mail* with detailed accounts of their visits, including a claim that Clinton had been flown to the island with his Secret Service contingent on a helicopter piloted by a woman who had just received her license, and that he had dinner with two underage "very innocent looking" girls. The problem with her story is that Secret Service and other records prove that none of the three had ever been on Epstein's island. It's also difficult to imagine a president being allowed to fly with an inexperienced pilot. Giuffre had simply made up the entire story for money, just as she made up the entire story about me.

It also turned out that Giuffre lied about her age and was well above the age of consent when she claims she was trafficked by Epstein. She originally claimed she was 14 when she first met Epstein and she vividly "remembered" celebrating her sweet 16th birthday with Epstein[7], but

---

6   These documents are quoted in subsequent chapters and reproduced in the Appendices.

7   On April 7, 2011, Giuffre told a lawyer that she was born on August 9, 1983, and that she first met Epstein "around June of 1998," which would have put her age at 14 years, 10 months. That was a lie. She didn't meet him until—at the earliest—mid-summer 2000, when she turned 17. She was also asked during that interview about several people associated with Epstein who might "have relevant information about Jeffrey's taking advantage of underage girls." When my name was offered, she said "yes." Of course, I would have such information, since I was one of Epstein's lawyers and such information was part of his guilty plea. I did not know of any of Epstein's unlawful activities before I became his lawyer. In this conversation, she did not accuse me of doing anything improper.

her own employment records conclusively proved she was 17 when she first met Epstein and her own statements show that she was close to 19 when she claimed Epstein "started to ask [her] to 'entertain' his friends." She later admitted these facts but said it was an honest mistake rather than a lie[8], despite her vivid, if demonstrably false, recollection about how she spent her sweet 16th birthday. Nonetheless, the media continues to refer to her as underage and to anyone who she claims had sex with her as a pedophile.

Exposing Giuffre's lies about her age is not intended to suggest that a 19-year-old cannot be abused by older men. It is intended only to case doubt upon her credibility with regard to her false claims against me. If she was, in fact, abused by others, she would be a victim even if she was above the age of consent. But her own Florida lawyer has cast doubt about whether she was forced to have sex with *any* prominent people.

The combined evidence of my innocence and her history of lying about her accusations and her age totally discredited her accusation against me.

It was not surprising, therefore, that the federal judge struck the accusation from the record as irrelevant and impertinent, and Giuffre's lawyers admitted that it had been a "mistake" to file it.

The matter was closed. I was exculpated by the evidence. The media, even the notorious social media, stopped accusing me. Life was back to normal. I was still controversial politically, especially because as a liberal Democrat who had strongly supported Hillary Clinton over Donald Trump, I was now defending President Trump's constitutional rights against those who would impeach or prosecute him. I wrote two controversial books on the subject and regularly appeared on TV. As a result, I became something of a pariah on Martha's Vineyard, where former friends turned against me for defending the constitutional rights of a president they honestly believed was bad for the country and the world. I was repeatedly asked how I could defend

---

8   In a recent interview with NBC News, Roberts said, "When you are abused, you know your abuser. I might not have my dates right, I might not have my times right… but I know their faces and I know what they've done to me." *Dateline* NBC, Sept. 20th, 2019.

the rights of a president I had voted against. Finally, my wife, who was getting bored with my complicated responses, got me a T-shirt that simply read: "It's the constitution, stupid." Wearing it didn't make me any friends. Nor did my advocacy for Israel make me many friends on the hard left. But even those who shunned and despised me for my defense of Trump's constitutional rights and my support for Israel did not believe that I had engaged in sexual misconduct.

My public life was more controversial than ever, but my private life returned to what it had been before the accusation against me had been proven totally false.

Then along came the #MeToo movement and everything changed. Although the evidence of my innocence only increased during this period[9]—and the evidence of my accuser's mendacity also became more evident—the atmosphere changed dramatically. Evidence was no longer important. It was the accusation that mattered, as well as the identities of the accuser and accused. The presumption shifted from innocence to guilt. For a man to call a false accuser a liar became a political sin, even if the accused had hard evidence of the accuser's lies, as I did. Much of the media, especially but not exclusively the social media, bought into the narrative of guilt by accusation instead of by proof. They refused to report on evidence of innocence that contradicted the narrative of guilt. For some an accusation of sexual guilt is so horrible that it must be true, regardless of the evidence. For others, it is irrelevant whether I did or did not have sex with Giuffre. I'm "guilty" of having defended Jeffrey Epstein, the porn star Harry Reems, the boxer Mike Tyson, and the football player O.J. Simpson, as well as having raised doubts about the credibility of some accusers. For these zealots, my history of defending a small number of accused rapists and wife-killers (even when combined with my history of representing many female victims) is enough

---

9   I had been warned that if I didn't withdraw a bar complaint I had filed against Giuffre's lawyers, they would get another woman to accuse me. The woman they found—who falsely claimed I had engaged in a threesome with her when she was 22 years old—admitted that she had "invented" false accusations against Epstein associates and others in order to frighten Epstein. She also invented the story about me, which was quickly discredited. More on this in subsequent chapters.

to overcome any presumption of innocence or absence of evidence of guilt.

In my case, as we shall see in detail in the pages to come, documents that were unlawfully hidden by my accuser and her lawyers were discovered and unsealed: they left no doubt that I had been framed for money. They proved Giuffre had never even met me in 2011—three years before she falsely claimed that in 2001 and 2002 she had engaged in sex with me on seven occasions. In 2011, she essentially admitted, in an exchange of emails, that she never had sex with me. And in a book manuscript she authored, she said she saw me once when she was nearly 19, "convers[ing] about business" with Epstein, but she did not include me among the men she named as having had sex with.

Giuffre's Florida lawyer, Bradley Edwards, also provided damning evidence that she lied about having been forced to have sex with many prominent people, including billionaire Leslie Wexner, former Israeli Prime Minister Ehud Barak, Senator George Mitchell, Ambassador Bill Richardson, and others. Edwards told a TV interviewer that based on his 11-year investigation, he does not believe that "any high profile people would be implicated," and that Wexner wasn't even aware of any sexual misconduct related to Epstein, and certainly didn't participate in any. If that is true, then Giuffre committed perjury.

These smoking-gun documents and recorded statements—which will be quoted in full and discussed in subsequent chapters—were barely mentioned by some media and not at all by most. Following the arrest and apparent suicide of Jeffrey Epstein, the media became even less willing to publish documented information that cast any doubt on the accounts of Epstein victims. In the minds of some, including some in the media, the presumption, indeed the certainty, of guilt that flows from an accusation by a woman cannot be overcome by evidence or the lack thereof. Though there is not a scintilla of evidence to support the accusation against me—no photographs, no witnesses, no documents, no contemporaneous accusation—and though the accuser has a long history of falsely accusing prominent men, and though she communicated to her friends she did not have sex with me, and though her lawyer admitted she was "wrong," the media persists in portraying me as possibly guilty.

The result of this media portrayal is that I am now presumed guilty—or at least suspect—and at age 81 my life and career are no longer being honored but dishonored. An obituary writer for the *Washington Post* called to tell me that he was drafting my obituary, which would include references to the accusation.[10] All this because of a demonstrably false accusation by a woman with a long history of lying.

* * *

If my evidence is not enough to overcome the current presumption of guilt by accusation, will any falsely accused person ever be able to prove his innocence?

I decided to write this book to address this question head on. Its title derives from a "demand" made by TV personality Meghan McCain that I not be allowed on TV because I was "accused" of sexual misconduct in the Epstein matter. The fact that I have disproved this false accusation is irrelevant to her. An accusation is enough to establish guilt in her mind and in that of other like-minded members of the media.

The current media cannot be trusted to tell the full story of a well-documented false accusation in this age of #MeToo and Epstein. As I will show, those few journalists who even try to be fair are accused of undermining the #MeToo movement.

So here is my story. I invite the readers to apply their critical skills to my evidence and arguments. I am confident that any fair assessment of the evidence and lack thereof will lead to only one conclusion: my accuser made up the entire false account to frame me for money and I

---

10   As *Slate* explained the process, "[N]ews organizations prepare so-called "advancers" in one of three situations: The subject is so famous that the paper would be embarrassed not to have an immediate package in the event of an untimely death; the subject is old or sick; or the subject is "at risk"—i.e., he's a drug addict or a stunt biker." Christopher Beam, Early Deadlines: How Far in Advance Do Newspapers Write Obituaries?, *Slate*, August 27, 2009. I hope I belong to the first rather than the second or third category.

am completely innocent. I know that for some, that will not be enough. I am writing this book despite my realization that it will probably be read largely by those who already know I'm innocent or who have an open mind about the issue. I have no expectation of opening the closed minds of zealots who believe that sexual assault is so heinous a crime that even total innocence should not be accepted as a defense.

I write as well for readers in future generations who may be more interested in the truth than some in the #MeToo generation seem to be. I write for my children, my grandchildren and their children. And I write to establish the historical and evidentiary record of my innocence. Eventually the pendulum will swing back to truth, and when it does, the documentation of my innocence will be available to those who care about what actually happened—and didn't happen.

Some friends and relatives have urged me not to write this book, because it will only continue the focus on the false accusation against me. They argue, quite persuasively, that the less attention paid to the accusation, the more likely the story will "go away." But it is not my goal to make the story "go away." My goal is to disprove it, categorically and definitively, until there is no lingering doubt in the minds of all fair and open-minded people.

They also argue that it is a fool's errand to try to "prove a negative"—namely, that I did not have sex with my accuser. It is, to be sure, a daunting challenge, but I accept it. If Giuffre had falsely accused me of having sex with her once in New York, it would have been nigh impossible to disprove that conclusively, even though it is untrue. But she foolishly accused me of having sex with her seven times in places her own lawyer admitted it would have been "impossible" for me to have been during the relevant time period. That, combined with her own implicit admissions—in the emails and manuscript—have made it possible for me to prove the negative.

Others have argued that my persistent claims of total innocence make me sound guilty. But if I remained silent—or simply issued a rote denial—some would say that my refusal to defend myself makes me "sound guilty." It's a no-win situation in the age of #MeToo. So I will continue to assert and prove my innocence—regardless of what some will say. All victims should speak out. Victims of sexual abuse as well as victims of false accusations of sexual abuse.

Finally, some have criticized me for calling my false accusers liars and perjurers, claiming that I am trying to "silence" victims of abuse. But it is my false accusers and their allies who have been trying to silence me, by calling me a pedophile and then saying that "accused" pedophiles should not have access to the media. They are also trying to silence me by threatening to sue and actually suing me for defamation if I defend myself against their false accusation in the court of public opinion.

To paraphrase Adlai Stevenson: If my accusers stop lying about me, I will stop telling the truth about them.

Hence this book.

Chapter 1

How I Met Jeffrey Epstein

I had never heard of Jeffrey Epstein when Lynn Forester—a prominent and wealthy woman who soon thereafter married Sir Evelyn Rothschild and became the Lady d'Rothschild—called and asked me to meet her "dear friend." I was on Martha's Vineyard with my family and was reluctant to have a guest, but Lynn implored me, saying it would be a great favor to her and that I would enjoy meeting this "wonderful and brilliant" man. She told me that he was interested in science and law, close to the president and provost of Harvard and a "good person." He and his friend Leslie Wexner had contributed a large sum of money to build the Hillel House at Harvard in honor of Harvard's Provost, Henry Rosovsky. Epstein was flying to the Vineyard to visit Lynn that day and she wanted to bring him over for a brief introduction. Lynn dropped him off at my house and he met my wife and children. We talked about science and his interest in funding some research at Harvard on evolutionary biology. I told him that I had taught a course with Stephen J. Gould, a world famous paleontologist and evolutionary theorist, and he asked me to introduce him to Steve.

Rothschild, herself a lawyer, had many prominent friends, including David Boies (about whom more later). She introduced many in her social circle to Epstein, including—she boasted—President Bill Clinton. She vouched for Epstein and became his calling card to people on the

Vineyard, in New York, in Palm Beach and elsewhere. Rothschild had a long-term, personal relationship with Epstein that ended in a financial dispute, amidst mutual recriminations over a townhouse she sold him for his friend Ghislaine Maxwell. Rothschild then told me that Epstein was "untrustworthy." (Epstein said the same about Rothschild.) But she did not tell me anything about his personal life.

Meeting Epstein was just about the worst thing that ever happened to me. I wish I had never laid eyes on him. I take full responsibility for becoming his acquaintance and lawyer, but I wish Rothschild had never asked me to meet him in the first place.

Shortly after our brief time together on the Vineyard, Epstein invited me to attend Leslie Wexner's 59th birthday dinner in New Albany, Ohio, a suburb of Columbus where Wexner had a mansion and several small houses on his property, including one owned by Epstein. He told me that Wexner, who was worth several billion dollars, did not want any material gifts for his birthday, but asked Epstein to bring the most interesting man he had met that year. Epstein said that he had told Wexner about me and Wexner wanted to meet me. I flew to New Albany on Epstein's private jet along with Senator and former astronaut, John Glenn, who was also a guest at the dinner party. The other guests included the former Prime Minister and soon to be President of Israel, Shimon Peres, as well as A. Alfred Taubman, the CEO of Sotheby's auction house. The all-male dinner was an intellectual as well as gastronomical feast. We discussed science, art, politics and Israel.

Shortly after this, Lynn Forester gave a birthday dinner for Rothschild on Martha's Vineyard. Epstein was there and so was Prince Andrew, the Duke of York. Forester introduced Epstein to all the fancy people in attendance and sang his praises.

At the dinner, Prince Andrew expressed an interest in attending my class at Harvard and I invited him to sit in on my first-year criminal law course. We were discussing the Second Amendment, and he raised his hand to make a point based on his own military experience with weapons. The dean then organized a faculty lunch in his honor. Several days later, he wrote me a letter of appreciation that included the following:

Dear Alan

Thank you for a most intellectual experience, it was fascinating insight into the law and the very serious subjects and dilemmas you face.

. . .

[T]he opportunity to be a student for just one lecture was an expanding experience and I cannot begin to thank you enough for your kindness.

Thanks must also be made for the fascinating tour of the Law School Library and the wonderful lunch with some of the faculty of Harvard. I was tempted to remain and enroll for a few other courses after the discussions at lunch! . . .

I look forward to continuing my intellectual challenge with you and Jeffrey E in the coming months. Thank you again for a fantastic experience.

Yours sincerely,

Andrew

The letter is dated 30 September 1999—a year before Giuffre met Epstein.

I then saw Epstein from time to time when he came to Harvard to meet with several faculty members and administrators to discuss academic issues. He introduced me to some Harvard professors whom I had never met, despite being on the same faculty for many years. Eventually Epstein established an office in Harvard Square where he invited faculty members from Harvard and MIT to participate in luncheon seminars, which I enjoyed immensely.

Epstein and I established an academic acquaintance, but never a close personal friendship. We never went out together socially. We did not discuss our families. I never met his mother or brother, or knew anything about them. Our relationship—one can call it a kind of friendship akin to that I had with other professional colleagues—centered around academic matters. He was interested in my writing and I sent him drafts of several books. His comments and critiques were insightful and interesting and I thanked him in my acknowledgments. He had street smarts and I enjoyed discussing my work with him. We never discussed his work, which remains something of a mystery beyond his money management for Leslie Wexner.

I attended several academic events at his home in New York and was invited—along with my nephew—to the launch of a manned space shuttle from the Kennedy Space Center.[11]

I never saw him in the presence of underage females or even anyone close to underage. While attending events at his home in New York—including one large party with Vera Wang, Amy Tan and other writers, artists and intellectuals—he introduced me and my wife to several of his women friends who were in their late 20s and early 30s. My wife didn't like Epstein's values, and especially his attitude toward women, but neither of us suspected that he had a penchant for teenagers. He kept that aspect of his private life completely separate from his academic friends.

In the late 1990s my wife, daughter and I were vacationing in the Caribbean and Epstein invited us to see the island he had recently bought. We spent a day there, dining with Professor Michael Porter of the Harvard Business School, his then-wife and their relatives. The island was empty, except for some staff and Epstein's erstwhile girlfriend Ghislaine Maxwell. While Epstein was working in his office, my wife had a massage from a professional massage therapist and my daughter and I explored the island. This was my only visit to Epstein's island, and it was well before he ever met Virginia Roberts Giuffre.

In an interview shortly after first being accused by Giuffre, I volunteered that I, too, had a massage from a professional therapist. Years later, the media tried to make a big deal of this, suggesting that I had "admitted" something devious. My massage, by a middle-aged woman of Russian background, had taken place well before Giuffre met Epstein and nearly a decade before anyone accused him of any improprieties. Epstein's house manager submitted a sworn affidavit in which he confirmed that my massage was by a professional therapist named Olga who "was in her forties." And, yes, I did keep my shorts on.

My family stayed in Epstein's Palm Beach home for several days in 2005 when my granddaughter participated in a soccer tournament

---

11 It was the launch of the *Atlantis* in 1997.

close by. Epstein was not there and the house was vacant except for the couple who took care of the house and prepared meals. I also stayed in his Palm Beach house when subsequently representing him and negotiating with the State Attorney of Palm Beach County. This was years after Giuffre separated from Epstein and moved to Australia. I flew in his small jet on several occasions on academic or legal business. The airplane manifests show that I was never on the plane with Giuffre or any underage females. I never heard the term "Lolita Express" used to describe the large jet he bought years later, until I read it in the press after he pleaded guilty. (Nor had I heard the term "pedophile" or "orgy" Island until after I began to represent Epstein. The island was called "Little Saint James," or jokingly "Little Saint Jeff." Epstein gave his guests sweatshirts with "Little Saint Jeff" printed on them.)

In none of these settings did I ever see an underage female, or even anyone close to underage. Nor did I ever see any photographs of nude or semi-nude women, or any sex toys. There were no clues that anything inappropriate had taken place in any of Epstein's homes. If there had been, I never would have allowed my children or grandchildren to have spent time there. Nor would the dozens of academics, journalists, business people or political figures who frequented his homes have remained silent. Epstein may have had inappropriate photographs and sex toys in his private bedroom areas but that was closed off to his prominent visitors, whom he was trying to impress with his academic and other connections.

My infrequent visits to Epstein's homes were no different from my visits to the homes of other academics and professional colleagues and friends, whose private areas I did not enter and into whose private lives I did not inquire.

* * *

As soon as Epstein was accused of sexual misconduct, my relationship with him changed completely. He asked me to become one of his lawyers and to help assemble a legal team, which I did. My relationship with him then became entirely professional. I billed him for every hour we spent together. Like many lawyer-client relationships, ours was tense and sometimes acrimonious. Nothing I did was good enough. He argued over my bills and whether I was prioritizing his case. Even the plea bargain we eventually struck—that the media labeled a "sweetheart deal"—did not satisfy him. "You should have done better," he complained.

The deal itself has been widely mischaracterized by the media. Prosecutors had a strong *state* case against Epstein. There was credible evidence that he had improper sexual contact with local underage girls whom he paid in cash. (His claim that the few underage girls had presented fake IDs was irrelevant under the law.) But that would not become a *federal* crime unless there was an *interstate* nexus: credible evidence that he had transported these girls across state lines or used interstate communications facilities for an improper purpose. Federal prosecutors could not prove these essential elements, so they agreed to a deal under which Epstein would plead guilty to a state crime, serve 18 months in jail, register as a sex offender and compensate all of his victims. The plea bargain represented the comparative strengths and weaknesses of each side: they had a strong *state*, but a weak *federal* case. We had strong defenses to a *federal* prosecution, but not to a *state* charge. Epstein pleaded guilty, served time in jail, registered as a sex offender and compensated his victims. My relationship with him then ended, except for an occasional phone call about the plea bargain. I was not aware of any of his personal activities after the plea bargain was finalized and implemented.

Let me be categorical and crystal clear and repeat here what I've stated under oath and subject to pain of perjury: during my changing relationship with Epstein—from academic acquaintance and colleague, to lawyer, to former lawyer—I never saw or did anything even remotely improper.

CHAPTER 2

"You've Been Accused"

———

O n the day before the 2015 New Year, I received a phone call from a journalist who said "You've been accused of having sex with an underage girl. What do you have to say?"[12]

I was shocked. I knew the accusation was false, because I had never had sex with an underage person, or with anyone other than my wife during the relevant time period. "Who, when, where?" I asked. The journalist told me the woman's name was Virginia Roberts Giuffre, who was then 32 years old. She claimed I had sex with her 16 years earlier, when she was 16 and being trafficked by Jeffrey Epstein. The woman who accused me was not among the alleged victims at the time of the plea bargain, but she was trying to join a lawsuit whose stated goal was to undo Epstein's plea agreement so she could sue him for a lot of money. As previously mentioned, I had been one of Epstein's lawyers—together with Kenneth Starr, Roy Black, and others—who had arranged a plea bargain under which Epstein pled guilty to two counts of solicitation and procuring. It was a controversial end to a highly publicized case, and many people were furious that an alleged predator received so "light" a sentence. Among those

———

12   The first story appeared in Josh Gerstein, Woman Who Sued Convicted Billionaire Over Sex Abuse Levels Claims at His Friends, *Politico*, Dec. 31, 2014.

who were most upset were some of his alleged victims, who were not notified in advance of the plea bargain.

I never met any of the alleged victims and knew nothing of the woman who was accusing me. It was an absurd accusation, and neither I nor my wife took it seriously. I joked that I had never had sex with an underage female—even when I was an underage male! My first marriage was when I was an inexperienced twenty-and-a-half-year-old, to my first serious girlfriend, whom I met in Jewish summer camp when I was sixteen-and-a-half. And in those days, there was no premarital anything among Orthodox Jews. A marriage license, unlike a driver's license, was not preceded by a learner's permit!

But within hours of learning of the false accusation, my phone began to ring and my inbox began to fill up, because I had been accused, along with Prince Andrew, in a court filing, which was leaked to the media. The story was being reported around the world, and although I generally received second billing to the prince, my name and that of Harvard were featured in many of the stories, generally in the headline.

* * *

My accuser initially insisted on anonymity in the lawsuit, even though she had given an interview in 2011 to a British tabloid, the *Daily Mail*, for which she was paid $160,000. In that article—in which she mentioned Prince Andrew and others, but not me—she had agreed to be named.[13] Consequently, the media quickly identified her, and I was told her name and shown her photograph, but neither was at all familiar to me. I was sure that I had never met her. I certainly had never had sex with her.

* * *

Giuffre never provided evidence beyond her own inconsistent words

---

13   Sharon Churcher, Teenage Girl Recruited by Paedophile Jeffrey Epstein Reveals How She Twice Met Bill Clinton, *Daily Mail*, March 5, 2011.

to support her allegations. Nor did she give dates—even months, seasons or years—when she claimed to have had sex with me. She and her lawyers simply threw my name into a court filing in a case in which I was not a party. It was as if she had scribbled my name on a bathroom wall, except that by including it in a court filing, she sought to obtain immunity from being sued for defamation. Also, by filing it in a court, she gave immunity to the media to publish it without doing any investigation, even if they didn't believe it was true, which several reporters told me they did not. The mere filing of the document made it "newsworthy" and protected it from defamation lawsuits.[14] She could, of course, have filed the accusation under seal, as she did regarding the numerous other people she accused—many of them prominent political and financial figures. But as I would later learn from Giuffre's best friend, the decision to accuse me in public, while accusing others in private, was part of a carefully calculated shakedown plot to get money from a wealthy individual who was not publicly named—at least not yet.

As soon as I learned of the false accusation, I agreed to respond to interview requests from major media around the world. I categorically asserted not only my complete innocence but also the physical impossibility of the allegations leveled against me: I had incontrovertible documentary evidence proving that during the relevant time period, I could not have been anywhere near four of the five locations where my false accuser said she had sexual relations with me. These

---

14 According to the Restatement (Second) of Torts, each party to private litigation is "absolutely privileged to publish defamatory matter concerning another preliminary to a proposed judicial proceeding, or in the institution of or during the course and as part of, a judicial proceeding in which he participates, if the matter has some relation to the proceeding." Restatement (Second) of Torts §588. As one scholar put it, "The rationale supporting the litigation privilege is that the integrity of the adversary system outweighs any monetary interest of a party injured by her adversary. The privilege has been noted to be "the backbone to an affective and smoothly operating judicial system." Eradicating the privilege "would dissuade attorneys from zealously representing their clients and might reduce access to courts." Louise Hark Hill, The Litigation Privilege: Its Place in Contemporary Jurisprudence, 44 Hofstra Law Review, 401-402 (2015) (internal citations omitted), The fair reporting privilege is a qualified privilege which immunizes a party from libel suits "for the publication of a fair and true report of any judicial proceeding, legislative proceeding or other official proceeding..." New York Civil Rights Section 74.

included a private Caribbean island, a New Mexico ranch, a Palm Beach mansion and a private jet all owned by Epstein. (The fifth was New York City, which tens of millions of people, including me, pass through.) I produced the evidence—travel, cell phone, credit card, and other records—that accounted for my whereabouts every single day of the two years during which this woman claimed she was being "trafficked" as a "sex slave."

A few days later, the *Wall Street Journal* published an op-ed entitled "A Nightmare of False Accusation That Could Happen to You"[15] in which I wrote about the legal predicament I found myself in and about the "gaping hole in our legal system" that permits unscrupulous individuals to make false accusations without any legal or pecuniary consequence. (More on this in Chapter 10.)

* * *

I agreed to waive the criminal statute of limitations by submitting a sworn affidavit that, if false, would subject me to a current perjury prosecution, despite the accusation being well beyond the statute of limitations. I challenged my accuser to produce any photographs or other physical evidence substantiating her account, which I knew could not exist. I also demanded that she and her lawyers repeat the accusation on TV, so I could sue them. Of course, they did not.

I called my false accuser a liar and perjurer—not only in court papers but in media interviews—knowing that this exposed me to the risk of an expensive and risky defamation suit by her.

In short, I did everything I would never allow any of my own clients to do—because most of my clients have had something to hide.

I've represented hundreds of individuals who have been accused of crimes ranging from mass murder to insider trading. Rarely have I known for certain whether they were guilty, innocent, or somewhere in between. In my first book written for a general audience, *The Best Defense*, published in 1982, I acknowledged that most of the criminal

---

15   Alan M. Dershowitz, A Nightmare of False Accusation That Could Happen to You, *Wall Street Journal*, Jan. 14, 2015

defendants I've represented have probably been guilty, because in the United States the majority of people charged with crimes "are in fact guilty." And thank goodness for that. No one would want to live in a country—like Iran or China—where a large number of innocent people are brought to trial. Although absolutely innocent people are sometimes charged with serious crimes, criminal justice systems that operate under the rule of law pride themselves on that happening quite rarely. So when I take a criminal case, I begin with a presumption of guilt: I assume my client probably did it, though I hope I'm wrong—and sometimes I am.

Generally, it is much safer for a criminal defense lawyer to presume guilt rather than innocence as a beginning hypothesis. If I were to presume my clients' innocence, I might make the mistake of allowing them to be questioned by the police. I might have them consent to a search of their home or computer. Or I might allow them to go on TV, assert their innocence, and lock in their account, which may turn out to be provably false.

If I were ever to have a case in which I knew for certain that my client was innocent—say I had a video of my client being on a different continent at the time of the crime—I might well waive his rights and encourage the police to question and search him. I might encourage him to go on TV, assert his innocence, tell his story, and even show the video. After all, if the client is innocent, what does he have to hide? Why have the client look guilty by refusing to answer questions?

Well, I was that client. Having nothing to hide, I did what I would never allow a client, of whose innocence I was not absolutely certain, to do. I went on TV, asserted my innocence, provided my evidence, waived the criminal statute of limitations and answered all questions.

I did it because I was my only client about whose absolute innocence there was no doubt. So I was prepared to break all of my rules, and the rules by which other good defense attorneys operate, when they represent accused persons of whose innocence they can never be absolutely certain. My candor and openness succeeded—at least initially.

The lawyers who filed the false accusation withdrew it and publicly acknowledged that it was a "mistake" to have filed sexual misconduct allegations against me.[16] An independent investigation by the former director of the FBI and former federal judge, Louis Freeh, concluded that there was no "evidence to support the accusations of sexual misconduct against [me]" that "in several instances, the evidence directly contradicted the accusations made against [me]," and "the totality of the evidence found during the investigation refutes the allegations made against [me]." (Appendix I) An investigation by James Patterson and two investigative reporters "found nothing other than accusations in terms of Dershowitz."[17]

One of the lawyers who had filed papers accusing me of having sex with Giuffre and other underage females—former federal judge and now a University of Utah law professor, Paul Cassell—acknowledged during a sworn deposition that he did not have the names of any such females, and had not spoken to any. In fact, he was not able to offer any actual evidence—because there was none—to corroborate his outrageous accusation. This is what he swore under oath when asked to name one of the other underage females with whom he said I may have had sex: "I have 24 names in mind as possible sexual abuse victims that Dershowitz *may or may not* have abused. And I have not been able to pinpoint exactly what happened." (Emphasis added.) He said that he got the names from a police report that referred to Jeffrey Epstein but *did not mention me*. It was a clear example of guilt by association between a client and his lawyer. The worst part was that this McCarthyite statement was not made by an ordinary lawyer but rather by a "distinguished" professor and former judge who lent his impeccable professional credentials to bolster the false accusations. Because he made it in a cowardly fashion behind the litigation privilege in a court proceeding, I couldn't sue him for defamation. He knew that if he made it outside of court, I would have sued him and won a large judgment. I challenged him then and invite him now to

---

16   This acknowledgement was part of a settlement between me and Giuffre's lawyer, ending defamation suits we brought against each other. They subsequently claimed they meant it was a "tactical" mistake, but that's not what the document says. See Chapter 6.

17   Jacob Gershman, James Patterson on Delving Into a Financier's Scandal in 'Filthy Rich,' *Wall Street Journal*, Oct. 8, 2016.

repeat his false and defamatory accusation outside of court. He won't. I also invite the Utah bar association to investigate his outrageous and unfounded accusation. They won't.

Not surprisingly, the federal judge before whom the false accusations were filed expressed outrage and struck them from the record as a "sanction" against the lawyers, and reminded the lawyers of their ethical obligations under court rules not to include irrelevant and impertinent accusations in court documents. But this positive result took many months, many dollars in legal fees, and considerable aggravation. It left lingering scars on my health and my reputation. It should never have happened, and it wouldn't have, had the lawyers representing Giuffre been more responsible and had the legal system not been unfairly skewed in favor of protecting those who level false accusations from behind the litigation privilege.

I am telling this story now so that the law may be reformed to protect innocent people from being falsely accused in the future. I am a victim of a false accusation, and I believe that victims must speak out against the injustices they suffered. The #MeToo movement has commendably forced into public view the rampant exploitation of vulnerable women by predatory men. Women who have been victims of sexual abuse must be encouraged to expose their abusers. But men who have been falsely accused—especially those, like me, who were deliberately targeted for crass financial gain—must also be encouraged to expose their false accusers. I will continue to speak out against anyone who has falsely accused me, despite the difficulty of proving one's innocence in the age of #MeToo. I will fight the current sexual McCarthyism of lawyers like Paul Cassell as strongly as I fought the political McCarthyism of my youth.

CHAPTER 3

David Boies and His Firm Create a Conflict of Interest

———

When I was first accused, one of David Boies's partners offered to represent me in my efforts to defend myself against the false charges leveled by Giuffre. I was not aware at the time that Boies had been representing Giuffre for several months before her accusation. It is a strange story, indeed, and one that raises important issues of legal ethics.

It began for me on January 22, 2015, when I appeared on the *Today Show* on NBC—ironically, interviewed by Matt Lauer, who three years later was fired by NBC for "inappropriate sexual behavior in the workplace"—and said the following:

> I've never seen her, I've never met her. . . . She is categorically lying and making the whole thing up. . . . I am afraid of nothing. I am hiding nothing. She is afraid of revealing this in public. She is afraid of giving dates or specifics. . . . I have been absolutely upfront in answering every question.

Later that day I received an email from one of Boies's partners, Carlos Sires, with whom I had worked on a case several years previously, along with another partner at the Boies Schiller & Flexner office in Fort Lauderdale, Sigrid McCawley. Sires said, "If there is anything I

can do for you, please let me know." Obviously, I didn't know that
his firm was already representing the woman who had falsely accused
me. Indeed, the partner who, along with Boies, was the key lawyer for
Giuffre, was Sigrid McCawley herself. I have no idea whether Sires
knew that his partner and friend was representing Giuffre when he
offered to represent me. I doubt it, since he told me on the phone call
that he "didn't believe" the accusations against me and he thought
the lawyers who had leveled them had "acted improperly." One of
those lawyers, it turns out, was David Boies, his senior partner.[18]

Sires told me that he would have to check with the managing
partner of the law firm before he could agree to represent me. That
is common, because lawyers always have to check to see that there is
no conflict of interest between clients they or their firm are representing. No conflict could be clearer than representing both the accuser
and the accused, without informing the accused. Later that evening
Sires sent me an email saying that he had checked with the managing
partner, Stuart Singer, that "Stuart and I think we can provide help,"
and that "Stuart and I look forward to working with you on this."
Sires also encouraged me to send written materials relevant to the
lawsuit that had been filed against me by Giuffre's lawyers. Based on
my reasonable assumption that they had done a conflict check and
that there was no conflict of interest in representing me, I responded
to Sires's request and had sent him material that would be necessary
to familiarize him with the case. Among the documents he received
was my detailed and highly confidential lawyer-client memorandum
which described the strategy I intended to pursue, including a tactical
step calculated to cause my opponents to fall into a legal trap. Sires
received, read, and commented on this highly confidential memorandum and sent me some additional material that he said might bolster
my position.

18 Sires was not the only lawyer to offer assistance when they heard that I was being
accused. Dozens of former students, colleagues, even strangers offered to join my legal
team. They included former judges, former prosecutors, and one former attorney general
of the United States. They were outraged at what they believed was irresponsible
behavior by the lawyers representing Giuffre. Ultimately, I put together a core legal
team, headed by my friend and colleague Kenneth Sweder, who guided me through the
complexities of the multiple litigations I faced as a result of the false accusation.

As far as I was concerned, Sires and the Boies law firm were my lawyers, with whom I could share important information that would be kept secret from my legal opponents. If I had known that the Boies firm was my opponent—that they were representing the very woman who had falsely accused me—I would certainly not have trusted them with my legal secrets.

* * *

Imagine my shock when I learned the truth. At first a member of the law firm told me that because Jonathan Schiller, one of the firm's name partners, was serving as chair of the Board of Columbia University, the firm was precluded from representing academics. That phony cover story didn't even pass the giggle test. I knew that wasn't the real reason, but had no idea what it was. When I found out the real reason—that they had long been representing my false accuser—I was furious at Boies, who was the responsible name partner. David and I had always been on good terms and I still find it hard to believe that two senior partners in his firm, including the managing partner of the Fort Lauderdale office, were offering to represent a well-known lawyer with whom Boies had a friendly relationship without being aware of the fact that he was representing my accuser. In fact, when Sires told me he had to check before agreeing to represent me, I told him that Boies and I were friends and offered to call him. Sires said that was unnecessary and that he would check with the managing partner in Florida. It is even more suspicious that McCawley, who was a partner in the same office as Sires, wouldn't know of his offer to represent me. She must have known that Boies was representing my accuser.

I have since learned that the Boies Schiller & Flexner firm (BSF) has been sanctioned many times for conflicts of interest. In 2013, for example, a judge for the United States District Court for the Southern District of New York ordered the Boies law firm to pay their opponent's legal fees on the grounds that "a clearer conflict of interest cannot be imagined. A first year law student on day one of an ethics course should be able to spot it. BSF, which holds itself out as one of the country's preeminent law firms, did not."[19] David Boies himself has also been involved in a number of conflict of interest situations. In 2005, Boies failed to disclose personal ties to three document companies to whom he had referred several clients.[20] More recently, the media reported that Boies was at the center of a conflict of interest involving his ethically incompatible roles as both a board member and lawyer for the fraudulent blood-testing company Theranos.[21] Also recently, Boies was representing *The New York Times* at the same time he was representing Harvey Weinstein and was involved in hiring investigators who were targeting the *Times* reporter in an effort to kill the story they were writing about Weinstein. The *Times* publicly fired Boies, calling his conflict of interest a "grave betrayal." Had I known BSF's sordid history—more of which is documented in Appendix A—when they offered to represent me, I would have been more suspicious and cautious.[22]

When I complained about this conflict of interest, Boies suggested that we talk. When we met in early 2015, he told me that he didn't know that Giuffre would be accusing me of sexual misconduct when he agreed to represent her. He said that he would never have agreed to represent her if he had had any idea that she would be accusing me. He also said that the lawyers who had included her allegations against me in the federal court filing "were wrong" to do so and had "a problem." He agreed to review my travel records, and if they supported my claim, he promised to try to persuade Giuffre that she had made a mistake in identifying me as one of the men with whom she had sex.

During 2015, Boies and I met several times in person in New York

19 Madison 92nd Street Associates LLC *v.* Marriott International, Inc. et al. (S.D.N.Y. Case No. 1:13-cv-00219_.

20 Robert Frank and Nathan Koppel, "Boies Office Sent Clients to 3rd Firm with Family Ties", *The Wall Street Journal*, October 11, 2005; Nathan Koppel, "Judge Orders Probe Into Boies Firm", *The Wall Street Journal*, February 8, 2006; Laurie P. Cohen and Robert Frank, "More Boies Clients Used Family Firm", *The Wall Street Journal*, August 31, 2005

21 Steven Davidoff Solomon, "Boies Dual Roles at Theranos Set Up Conflict, *New York Times*, February 2, 2016

22 In addition to these and other conflicts, Boies and his firm have been credibly accused of numerous other ethical violations, some of which are catalogued in Appendix A.

for many hours, reviewing the evidence. We spoke on the phone more than a dozen times. After reviewing my travel and other records, he acknowledged that it would have been "impossible" for me to have been at the various locations in which his client claimed to have had sex with me during the entire two-year time period during which Giuffre knew Epstein. Giuffre refused to be specific about times within that period, especially after she learned that I had detailed records of my whereabouts. The records proved conclusively that I had never set foot on Epstein's island, ranch, Palm Beach estate or airplane during the two years Giuffre claimed to have been having sex with me in those places. I had, of course, been in New York, but Boies assured me this was irrelevant, since "everyone passed through New York" and since it was clear that I could not have been in the other locations in which Giuffre had accused me with great specificity. Boies and his partner, McCawley, spent hours with me and my paralegal, Nicholas Maisel, on two separate occasions reviewing the records. I memorialized what he told me in contemporaneous notes, quoting his exact language. (Appendix B) In the presence of several other lawyers, Boies repeatedly stated that he was convinced that I could not have been in the locations during the relevant time period. Here is what he said: "It looks to me like this set of dates would make it impossible for you to have been on the island or at the ranch during the relevant time." He promised that unless Giuffre acknowledged that she was mistaken about me, and withdrew the accusations she had made in the court papers, he would have no choice but to terminate his representation of her. He promised to arrange a meeting with Giuffre and get back to me. But he kept making excuses for not meeting with her.

Once I realized Boies would not keep his word, I recorded several conversations with him. (Recording is legal in New York if one party consents.)[23] Here are his and my exact words, as recorded (and confirmed by law enforcement officials):

---

23 New York is a "one-party consent" state, which means New York makes it a crime to record a telephone conversation unless one party to the conversation consents. See N.Y.Penal Law §§ 250.00, 250.05.

. . .

Dershowitz: You're as persuaded as we are that it was not possible for me to be on the island to have sex with her in New Mexico on the airplane and Palm Beach. But New York as you say, is a little bit up in the air. What is the next step at this point?

Boies: I think the next step would be for me and Sigrid, both of us together, to sit down with our client and say explicitly: 1) "We know you believe that you had relations with Professor Dershowitz. We have taken steps to share some of the [unclear] You understand to get an honest opinion. However, we have now reviewed the documentary evidence and we are convinced that your belief is wrong and we would like to explore with you how you could have come to this conclusion [unclear]. We have some ideas [unclear]. It is not surprising to me, how you could have, at your age and under the circumstances that you were under at the time, have misidentified somebody or perhaps had somebody intentionally misidentify him for you. The former is more likely than the latter. But there are certainly a number of possible explanations and I'd like to review that with you and help you try to explore how you could have come to that conclusion [unclear] One thing is clear—your conclusion is simply wrong.

In subsequent phone calls, he repeated his acknowledgment that Giuffre was "wrong" and that her claim is "unsustainable."

I filed a sworn affidavit quoting those words, but without saying I had them on tape. *The New York Times* reported my account and asked Boies for his response. Here is what he said: "I never said to him that I concluded that my client's assertions were incorrect. . . . I didn't say that. *I didn't say anything like that.*"[24] (Emphasis added.) Of course this wasn't true: he had said precisely that in our recorded conversations, and lied to *The New York Times*. I challenged him to repeat his false

---

24   Barry Meier, Alan Dershowitz, on the Defense (His Own), *New York Times*, Dec. 12, 2015.

denial under oath, warning him that he would be committing perjury if he did. He subsequently filed a declaration in which he said: "Much of what Mr. Dershowitz asserts in his Affidavit is misleading, taken out of context, or flatly untrue"—a weaselly formulation apparently calculated to avoid a perjury charge. Boies definitely did tell me that his client was "wrong" when she identified me as someone with whom she had had sex, and the evidence that Giuffre was wrong about me has only gotten stronger since Boies made that admission.

If Boies had any doubts about the credibility of his client, he could have easily resolved them with one phone call. Giuffre had told the media that she had met former vice president Al Gore and his wife Tipper on Epstein's notorious island. She described the meeting in considerable detail as early as 2011, in her $160,000 *Daily Mail* interview:

> Virginia disclosed that Mr. Clinton's vice-president Al Gore and his wife, Tipper, were also guests of Epstein on his island. . . . "The Gores seemed like a beautiful couple when I met them. All I knew was that Mr. Gore was a friend of Jeffrey's and Ghislaine's. Jeffrey didn't ask me to give them a massage. There might have been a couple of other girls there on that trip but I could never have imagined this guy would do anything wrong. I was planning to vote for him when I turned 18. I thought he was awesome."[25]

She also wrote the following in the manuscript for the book she was planning to publish:

> I met Al Gore and his lovely wife during one of those many weekends away in the Caribbean. I was blown away by the amount of attention Al doted on his wife, it was so sweet to watch. They sat next to each other at the dinner table gazing into one another's eyes having an intimate conversation between them. Among the many guests visiting that night and many of them young beautiful women, not once did Al's eye's stray elsewhere, to them they were

25 Sharon Churcher, Teenage Girl Recruited by Paedophile Jeffrey Epstein Reveals How She Twice Met Bill Clinton, *Daily Mail*, March 5, 2011. See Appendix M.

the only ones there. He was up for a presidential election that year and he definitely had my vote. Anyone that could show that much devotion and passion towards his loved ones could have the same devotion towards running a country, or at least I thought so. He only left his wife's side to have a walk down to the beach with the host of the weekend, Jeffrey.[26]

The problem is that neither Gore nor his wife had ever been on Jeffrey Epstein's island. They didn't know Jeffrey Epstein. They had never even met him. Giuffre had made up the entire detailed and vivid account in order to sell newspapers and a book.

* * *

David Boies had represented Al Gore in the 2000 election case. Boies could easily have picked up the phone and called Gore. If he had, Gore would have told him categorically that Giuffre was not telling the truth when she described her fictional encounter with him. I specifically asked Boies to call Gore, but he said it wasn't necessary because he was already convinced she was mistaken about me, and her general credibility was not at issue. But, of course, it was. If she deliberately lied about Gore to sell her story, she would certainly not hesitate to lie about me to obtain even more money.

Having been caught lying about meeting the Gores on Epstein's island, Giuffre has compounded and updated her lie by now admitting she may be wrong about where she met them, but not about having met them somewhere with Epstein, perhaps in New York. But the Gores were never with Epstein anywhere. Moreover, Giuffre described in detail seeing Al Gore "walk down the beach" with Epstein on his Caribbean island. Pure fantasy!

Giuffre had also invented a story about having dinner with

---

26 These memoirs were recently unsealed and are available at https://assets. documentcloud.org/documents/6251258/Virginia-Roberts-Memoir.pdf. This passage can be found on p. 109. See Appendix G.

President Bill Clinton on Epstein's Island. Here is her vivid, but completely invented account:

> "I'd have been about 17 at the time. [Giuffre turned 17 in August of 2000, while Clinton still had nearly half a year left in his Presidency.] I flew to the Caribbean with Jeffrey and then Ghislaine Maxwell went to pick up Bill [Clinton] in a huge black helicopter that Jeffrey had bought for her.
>
> She's always wanted to fly and Jeffrey paid for her to take lessons, and I remember she was very excited because she got her license around the first year we met.
>
> I used to get frightened flying with her but *Bill had the Secret Service with him* and *I remember him* [Clinton] *talking about* what a good job she did.
>
> We all dined together that night. Jeffrey was at the head of the table. Bill was at his left, and I sat across from him. Emmy Tayler, Ghislaine's blonde British assistant, sat at my right. Ghislaine was at Bill's left and at the left of Ghislaine there were two olive-skinned brunettes who'd flown in with us from New York.
>
> I'd never met them before. I'd say they were no older than 17, very innocent-looking."[27] (emphasis added)

Secret Service and other records prove that Clinton was never on the island. Moreover, it's hard to imagine Secret Service agents flying with Clinton on a helicopter piloted by a woman who had just gotten her license. Giuffre invented these false accounts, just as she invented the false accounts of meeting me.

Recently, after this preposterous account was debunked, Giuffre invented a new account: she claimed that she didn't tell the reporter that she "remembered" Clinton telling her what a good job Maxwell did (despite these words being quoted, not paraphrased); she now says that Sharon Churcher misquoted her and that it was Maxwell, not Clinton, who told her that, and Maxwell may have been lying to

27 Sharon Churcher, Teenage Girl Recruited by Paedophile Jeffrey Epstein Reveals How She Twice Met Bill Clinton, *Daily Mail*, March 5, 2011.

her. She did not correct the alleged "error" at the time it was published. Yet another lie to add to her long list of fabrications.

As previously proven, Giuffre also lied about being underage when she claims to have been trafficked. Her own employment records and a manuscript of a book she wrote prove that she lied about being below the age of consent when she said she had sex with prominent people. She originally said that she vividly remembered spending her "sweet 16: birthday celebration with Epstein,"[28] but her employment records prove—and she now concedes—that she didn't meet Epstein until a year after she turned 16, and that she was well above the age of consent when she claims to have had sex with Epstein's friends. (Appendix G)

In her first interview about Epstein at the beginning of 2011 with the *Daily Mail*—the closest in time to the alleged events and before she was "pressured" by her lawyers—this is what she said: "Basically I was training to be a prostitute for him and his friends who shared his interest in young girls . . . *After about two years* he started to ask me to 'entertain his friends.'"[29] (Emphasis added.) This chronology would put her close to 19—well above the age of consent—when she entertained her first "clients" on Epstein's island, not 16 as she first mendaciously claimed.

Giuffre's lawyers had to be aware of her history of lying when they vouched for her credibility by submitting perjured affidavits by her falsely accusing me of sexual misconduct with her.

On October 16th, 2019, Federal Judge Loretta Preska disqualified the entire Boies law firm from representing Giuffre in her defamation suit against me on several grounds, including that Boies will be called as a witness and asked about his recorded admission that Giuffre was "wrong . . . simply wrong" in accusing me. She found that disqualification was "clearly required" under the law.

---

28 Giuffre's Memoirs, p. 40 ("I spent my sweet 16th birthday on [Epstein's] island in the Caribbean . . ."). See Appendix G.

29 Tom Leonard, Prince Andrew Risks Losing Ambassador Job As Girl in Underage Sex Case Reveals Meeting Him, *Daily Mail*, March 2, 2011.

CHAPTER 4

The Chronology of a Frame-up; The Newly Unsealed Emails and Manuscript

The recent unsealing of documentary evidence has made it clear how Giuffre's story about me evolved—from never having met or having sex with me, which is the truth, into a false accusation of having sex with me in numerous places I couldn't have been during the relevant time period. We have evidence that Giuffre never accused me of having had sex with her until she met her lawyers, who must have told her she would get a big payday if she accused me. Her best friend, a woman named Rebecca Boylan, has said in a recorded statement that she "never heard [Giuffre] mention [Dershowitz] as someone with whom she had sex," and that Giuffre didn't want to include my name in the legal pleadings even after she retained her lawyers, but she "felt pressured" by her lawyers to name me. (Appendix C)

During the two-year period she was with Epstein—between 2000 (when she was seventeen) and 2002 (when she was nineteen)—she told several people that she was being paid to have sex with prominent individuals. Among the people she told was her then-boyfriend, Anthony Figueroa. He, too has confirmed that she never mentioned me as someone with whom she'd had sex. In a sworn statement, Figueroa stated that:

"Virginia only mentioned Alan Dershowitz, as she was listing famous people who were friends of Jeffrey Epstein. I remember during
this same conversation she listed certain famous people like President Clinton, Kevin Spacey, and Chris Tucker. Virginia described
Mr. Dershowitz as 'OJ Simpson's lawyer.' She did not say she had
ever had any physical contact with him. As I have said before, she
had never mentioned anything about them having sex, or brought
up anything like that. The first time I heard about Virginia's sexual
allegations against Mr. Dershowitz was after the court filing in January 2015 when the media started to contact me for interviews."
(Appendix D)

Moreover, Epstein's house manager during the relevant time period,
Juan Alessi, swore under oath that he never saw me in the presence of
"young girls" and never saw me do "anything improper." (Appendix E)

* * *

When Giuffre was interviewed by federal agents in 2013, she accused
others but not me. (Appendix F) Moreover, there is documentary
proof that the U.S. Attorney's office did not consider me to be an ac-
complice to Mr. Epstein's alleged crimes: the Assistant U.S. Attorney
listed the people involved in criminal activity in the Epstein matter but I was not among them. Had there been any suspicion or any
involvement on my part in sexual improprieties, prosecutors would
never have permitted me to serve as Epstein's lawyer and participate
in negotiating the plea bargain.

The first time my name was publicly mentioned as someone to
whom Giuffre was trafficked was in the legal filings on December 30,
2014,[30] months after Giuffre met Boies and her other lawyers, who, according to Rebecca Boylan, pressured her into including me in order to
obtain money from Leslie Wexner, the billionaire owner of Victoria's

---

30 Jane Doe # 1 & Jane Doe #2 v. U.S., Case No. 08-80736-Civ-Marra/ Johnson,
United States District Court Southern District of Florida, available to view at https://
online.wsj.com/public/resources/documents/2015_0102_epsteindershowitz.pdf

Secret and other companies. We now have smoking-gun documents produced in the defamation lawsuit between Giuffre and Maxwell that had been placed under seal but have now been unsealed. Here is the story of this effort by Giuffre's lawyers to suppress the damning truth about how Giuffre came to falsely accuse me.

During the defamation suit between me and Giuffre's lawyers, Brad Edwards and Paul Cassell, I subpoenaed all emails from and to Giuffre that mentioned my name. The judge ordered all such emails to be produced, but they were improperly withheld. Giuffre was then directly asked whether there were any such emails. With her lawyer sitting next to her, she brazenly lied under oath and swore there weren't. Well, there were. And they were dynamite. They have now been unsealed and it is obvious why she and her lawyers failed to disclose them.

The first email was in May 2011, from Giuffre to a journalist named Sharon Churcher, who was helping her sell a book she was writing about her sexual experiences in connection with Epstein. This is what the first email said:

> "Hi, Sharon, . . . Were[sic] drawing up a contract through her agent right now and getting busy to meet my deadline. Just wondering if you have any information on you from when you and I were doing interviews about the JE story . . . I wanted to put the names of some of the assholes, oops, I meant to say, pedo's that J.E. sent me to. With everything going on, my brain feels like mush and it would be a great deal of help!"

Churcher responded with the following email:

> "Don't forget Alan Dershowitz . . . J.E.'s buddy and lawyer . . . good name for your pitch as he repped Claus von Bulow and a movie was made about that case . . . title was *Reversal of Fortune*. We all

suspect Alan is a pedo and tho no proof of that, you probably met him when he was hanging put[sic] w JE."[31]

Giuffre's reply did not dispute Churcher's "no proof" statement. All it said was, "Thanks again Shazza, I'm bringing down the house with this book."[32]

Giuffre then followed Churcher's advice and put me in her manuscript. But—and here is the key—she put me in the manuscript as someone with whom she did NOT have sex. This is significant because in the same manuscript she included detailed descriptions of the people with whom she says she DID have sex. (Appendix G) These men included included "A powerful Senator George Mitchell," "Alexandra Cousteau, the granddaughter [of] Jack [sic] Cousteau," "Glena and Eva," "Ron Eppinger," and "A professor named Stephen _____." His last name has been redacted from the unsealed material, but I know who he is. This is how Giuffre described her encounter with him, as her second client:

> "Two weeks later, as if Jeffrey was trying to lighten my spirits, he told me I would be going to his island to meet a new client. He is a Harvard Professor, named Stephen [redacted]. I would be spending two days with him showing him around the island, dining with him, and treating him to a massage whenever he wanted. Without Jeffrey even verbalizing the need to have sex with him, he told me to keep him happy like I had my first client. . . .
>
> Stephen was a quirky little man with white hair and a mad scientist look about him. . . . We made our acquaintances and he looked as if he was tripping over himself with words, obviously delighted with his company and location for the weekend. I showed him around as Jeffrey had asked and took him on an adventurous quad bike ride around the small curvy paths, leading the way and letting loose my hair, doing something that gave me a natural high instead of the

---

31   These exchanges have been reproduced in several media outlets, including Tracy Connor, Alan Dershowitz: Unsealed Emails Show Epstein Accuser Lied About Sex With Me, *Daily Beast*, Aug. 20, 2019.

32   See Appendix K.

prescription one. The sights alone were breathtaking from the mountainous peaks of the untouched parts of the island, we sat at a cliff and just sat there, not saying a word to each other besides to compliment the sights mother nature that appealed to us. I didn't feel as if I owed this stranger anything but what was expected of me by Jeffrey and I could be polite, I just couldn't be myself. . . .

We both met at six pm for dinner on the outside veranda. . . We both drank the red wine supplied on the table and it seemed to warm me up on the breezy night. By the time dinner was served and another red wine bottle later, he seemed to get funnier. I made fun of his tousled hair and he poked me for my skinny legs, calling me a wanna-be-anorexic. When dessert was brought out, he asked if he could receive one of the delightful massages he has been hearing about from Jeffrey. I gulped more red wine down and sweetly complied with his offer, dreading the moment I'd have to see his naked body let alone touch it. I asked the housekeeper Kathy that had been serving us that night to please have someone set up a massage bed in one of the cabana's. I went to my room to down a few Xanax, telling him I wanted to freshen up after dinner, but to meet me in his cabana in twenty minutes or so. I was ready to go as I had said, twenty minutes later, with the effects of the tablets mixed with the red wine, and I would be free not to feel anything. He was still dressed when I got in the cabana obviously not accustomed to this and a lot shyer than what I had been used to, I told him he'd need to undress and lie face down on the table, putting a towel to cover his bare bottom to prevent him feeling embarrassed during the massage. I gave the massage my earnest as I always had, and quickly got through having intercourse with him. Not wanting to make any foreplay or anything extravagant out of it, I let him think that's as good as it got, and by the smile on his face, I thought I had done enough.

The next day I took him down to the beach for a real massage under tiki-hut on the water's edge. It was one of Jeffrey's favorite places to have a massage, as he droned out to the sound of the waves and my gentle therapeutic strokes. Afterwards we had lunch back at the main villa and went back down to the beach to swim out to the water trampoline about one hundred meters off the dock. He didn't do any bounding around or anything like that. It was just a good base point for a rest spot after a long swim. What was really cool about it though, was you could see through the mesh and watch fish swimming underneath. . . .

I asked him if he'd like another massage before I went to bed. He just wanted to stay up watching movies in Jeffrey's theatre room. . . . The next morning, we were both catching a flight from St. Thomas and we had no time for anything other than breakfast and packing, which saved me from having to be too polite as we said our good-bye's from the terminal in the airport, both hurriedly off in separate directions, thankfully. I arrived back in Palm Beach, only to be told to catch another flight the next day to N.Y.C. where Jeffrey would fix me up the money he owed me for treating his colleague out to an entertaining weekend."

In her manuscript Giuffre also described sexual encounters with an MIT professor, several politicians and businessmen. (Appendix G) If she had had sex with me, she surely would have included me in this catalogue of alleged criminals, especially since the journalist had told her that including me would help her pitch the book. But here is everything she wrote about me:

"Alan Dershowitz, his colleague in finances and personal solicitor, a bird of the same feather I had seen hanging around the island and Jeffrey's Manhattan mansion, more and more these days. Alan's taste for the young and beautiful was a bias [sic] for a blooming business relationship between him and Jeffrey. After an explicit session of Jeffrey's vulgar pilgrimage into my body, we were interrupted by a knock at the door by Jeffrey's good friend, Alan. . . .. Opening the bedroom door and letting Alan inside they began to converse about business immediately, right in front of me. Jeffrey started to tell Alan what needed to be done while he jostled some notes down quickly. I peeked my head from underneath the covers thinking they were too wrapped up in their work to notice me get up and dressed, and Jeffrey turned back to me and told me to just stay there this would only take a second. Going back to Alan he turned his focus back into work and hustled out a few more orders before letting Alan out of the door and returning his attention to me."[33]

Giuffre made up this entire story. My records prove that I was never on the island during the time she knew Epstein. I had no "business relationship" with Epstein—this was years before I became his defense attorney—and was never in his bedroom. But the crucial point is that Giuffre did not make up a false claim that she had sex with me, even when she was inventing a story about seeing me. This is especially striking since she said I had a "taste for the young and beautiful," and Churcher had said that "we all suspect Alan is a pedo." If I had done anything that confirmed these false suspicions, Giuffre would surely have included it.

Why would she write in detail about a sexual encounter with an obscure professor named Stephen whom no one has ever heard of, if she could help pitch her book by including a sexual encounter with a far more famous professor? This only plausible answer is that it never occurred to her to invent a sexual encounter with me that had never taken place—until she felt pressure to include me by her lawyers. She only began to invent the false sex accusation against me after she met with lawyers and learned that she could profit from including me. Even then she didn't want to name me, because she knew it wasn't true, but succumbed to the pressure from her lawyers and agreed to make up the story about me. She then essentially substituted me for Professor Stephen, whom she had described in the manuscript, and perhaps for others. To make her story consistent, she then had to testify that she *never had sex* with Professor Stephen, despite having vividly described her days with him in the manuscript. She surely could not have forgotten spending so much time with her second client.

This chronology is confirmed by what she told the FBI, her former boyfriend and her best friend before she was pressured by her lawyers: namely, that I was not among the men she was accusing. It has also been confirmed by Sharon Churcher—the first journalist to interview

---

33   Roberts Manuscript, p. 112

Giuffre back in 2011. In Churcher's numerous interviews, Giuffre never included me in the "laundry list" of men with whom she said she had sex. That's why Churcher wrote that there was "no proof" that I did anything wrong. Churcher has now said that she doesn't believe Giuffre's accusations against me and that I am "a victim" of a false accusation influenced by Giuffre's lawyers and/or money.[34]

Giuffre has now come up with another lie to "explain" why these damning emails and manuscript do not prove that she made up the entire story of having sex with me. She claims that her manuscript was intended to be a "fictionalized account"—a "novel"—rather than a factual account of what actually happened.[35] This is utter nonsense, as proved by the indisputable fact that the account she provided to the FBI—under penalty of lying to law enforcement officials—precisely paralleled what she wrote in her manuscript. She also asked Churcher for the actual "names" of the "pedo's that J.D. sent me too." She then included *the actual names* of those she was accusing— and did not include me. If the manuscript was intended to be fiction, rather than fact, why would she risk defamation suits by naming those she was accusing? And if it was fiction, why was she willing to falsely accuse those who she named? Another lie by a woman who truly doesn't understand the differences between fiction and fact.

Here, then, in summary form is how Giuffre's story evolved:

- 2011: Giuffre is interviewed by Churcher about her sexual encounters. She mentions numerous men, but not me.
- 2011: She had to be told by Churcher that I wrote *Reversal of*

---

34 Sharon Churcher has said that her lawyer has publicly confirmed that Giuffre never had sex with me. We are currently seeking to unseal a brief filed by Churcher's lawyer that confirms Churcher's exculpatory assessment.

35 In a court submission in the defamation case, Giuffre v. Maxwell, Roberts claims that "in 2011, she sought psychological counseling from a psychologist for the trauma she endured... Also that year, journalist Sharon Churcher sought her out, and traveled half way around the globe to interview her on painful subjects. [She] began to draft a *fictionalized* account of what happened to her... Doing so was an act of empowerment and a way of reframing and taking control over the narrative of her past abuse that haunts her." (Emphasis added.)

Fortune and am famous and would be a "good name for your pitch."

- 2011: Churcher tells Giuffre, "you probably met him" hanging around with Epstein, though there is "no proof" he did anything wrong.

- 2012 Manuscript: Giuffre said she saw me in Epstein's bedroom discussing business with Epstein, but not that she ever actually met me or had sex with me.

- 2013: Giuffre tells the FBI about the men with whom she says she had sex. She does not include me. She also tells James Figueroa (her then-boyfriend) and Rebecca Boylan (her childhood best friend) whom she met and had sex with, but does not include me.

- 2014: Meets her lawyers, who, she tells Rebecca Boylan, pressured her to include me among people with whom she had sex.

- 2014-2015: After meeting with her lawyers—and "feeling pressure" from them—Giuffre suddenly "remembers" having sex with me seven times between 2001 and 2002 (when she was 18 and 19). She substitutes me for Professor Stephen in her new false account, and then denies having sex with him, despite her vivid description of her sexual encounter with him in her manuscript.

- 2015-2019: Her lawyers are well aware of this chronology and these facts when they submit perjured affidavits by her, falsely accusing me of having had sex with her.

CHAPTER 5

Suitable for Framing; Why Me?

During my interviews with the media, I was frequently asked the following questions: Why would Giuffre accuse you if it wasn't true? What does she have to gain by accusing you?[36] She had to know you would fight back. I too was puzzled by these questions.

As soon as I heard of the false accusation against me, I suspected that it was about money. Giuffre claimed in her filings that in addition to Prince Andrew and me, she had engaged in sex with numerous "politicians, powerful business executives, foreign presidents, a well-known Prime Minister, and other world leaders." Ultimately she named many of these individuals, but only in a sealed deposition. Even before her testimony was unsealed, my own investigation established that they included former Senate Majority Leader George Mitchell, former cabinet member Bill Richardson, the late MIT Professor Marvin Minsky, a wealthy hotel owner from the Pritzker family, billionaire Leslie Wexner, former Israeli Prime Minister Ehud Barak and other well-known, respected and

---

36 This attitude that "women need to be believed" because the women have "nothing to gain" by accusing someone of sexual assault dominated the Kavanaugh hearings. At the time of the controversial confirmation hearings, I wrote several op-eds urging the public not to make decisions who to believe based on gender identity, including "How To Decide Who To Believe in Kavanaugh, Rosenstein Drama," *The Hill*, Sept. 25, 2018, and "Postpone Kavanaugh Confirmation Until FBI Can Investigate Accusations Against Him," Fox News, Sept. 27, 2018.

wealthy figures. Why then did she only name me and Prince Andrew in a public filing and the others in sealed filings? I soon began to suspect that I was being used as a stalking horse in a scheme to obtain money from at least some of these as-yet publicly unnamed wealthy alleged abusers. I believed that the not-so-subtle threat message to these unnamed but privately accused individuals was that if they did not want to have happen to them what had happened to me—namely, to have their names spread all over the world as accused pedophiles—her silence could be bought for a price, just as her public accusations made to the *Daily Mail* against Prince Andrew, President Clinton and Vice President Gore and his then-wife Tipper had been bought for a price. As I later testified, I believed it was an encouragement to the unnamed individuals to "pay money for [their names] not being mentioned or revealed."

* * *

I knew that I was *not* the likely target of the plot for several reasons: first, the target of blackmail from whom the money is sought isn't publicly revealed, because it is *the threat* of public disclosure that is held over the head of the target; second, anyone who knows me would realize that I would never pay a penny to buy the silence of a false accuser; and finally, nobody had asked me for money. (That has since changed.) It seemed logical that the false accusation against me was being used to pressure someone else. At least that is what I believed. But I had no idea who it could be. I knew it had to be someone wealthy who was acquainted with Jeffrey Epstein. Epstein had many rich friends, and it could be any or all of them.

* * *

Then suddenly, out of the blue, I found out. Giuffre's longtime best friend, a woman named Rebecca Boylan[37], reached out to me through

---

37 Until now, I have not disclosed Rebecca's last name, because she didn't want to be called by journalists, but the media has now found her, disclosed her name and tried to interview her.

her husband. She was reluctant to become involved, but felt terrible about what was happening to me. She had just spent time with her friend Virginia after Virginia had been beaten up by her husband. They discussed me in some detail. Boylan told me that Giuffre had never previously mentioned me as one of the people with whom she claimed to have had sex and that she didn't want to accuse me in the legal papers, but she "felt pressure" from her lawyers to include me. Boylan's husband confirmed that Giuffre had told them I was *not* among the men with whom she had sex.

Then Boylan told me who she believed the real target was: she didn't know his name, but she knew he was a wealthy businessman from Ohio who owned the Limited Too and Victoria's Secret. I immediately knew she was referring to Leslie Wexner, who was a close friend and longtime business associate of Jeffrey Epstein. Boylan gave me permission to record our conversation, and this is what she told me:

> She [Virginia Roberts Giuffre] just said that he owned Victoria's Secret and Limited Too, and that he had lots of money. You know, was a billionaire. . . . They wanted to sue him for at least half his money. . . . She made it sound like they were already talking to him and they were . . . already, you know, in the process of suing him. . . . She also said to me that . . . when it came to Alan Dershowitz that she did feel pressure to go after you . . . she felt pressure to do it, she didn't want to go after you specifically, that she felt pressured by her lawyers to do that.

Boylan also told me that:

> "Virginia never wanted to go after you but she felt pressured by her lawyers. I never heard her mention you when we were kids or until very recently when things happened in the media. But I never heard her mention you before."

I immediately called Leslie Wexner to inform him that he might be the target of a plot to threaten him with public exposure unless he paid money to buy Giuffre's silence. I reached his wife, Abigail, who confirmed that Giuffre's lawyers had been in touch with them about what she characterized as a "shakedown." She referred me to their lawyer, John Zeiger. I called Zeiger, who confirmed that Giuffre's lawyers had contacted him. He, too, used the world "shakedown." Boies had secretly reached out to Wexner, at about the same time my name had been made public, and later met with Zeiger.

Boies's co-counsel, Stanly Pottinger, has stated in an affidavit that Giuffre had asserted that Wexner "had sex with one or more of Epstein's girls, including Mrs. Giuffre." (See Appendix J.)

Zeiger told me that Boies had informed him that his client, Virginia Roberts Giuffre, was accusing Wexner of having had sex with her on multiple occasions while she was underage. The accusation was strikingly similar to the one made against me, in terms of location, frequency, and other details. But there was one significant difference: Giuffre was also accusing Wexner of having made her dress up in baby-doll lingerie of the kind sold by Victoria's Secret. If this accusation were to be made public, it would have a devastating impact on the company and on Wexner's leadership of it.

Wexner's lawyers told Boies that the accusations were absolutely false. They also noted that any claims were well beyond the statute of limitations that then governed, since they were alleged to have occurred nearly fifteen years earlier. Why, then, would Boies take time out of his very busy schedule to pursue a legal case that was barred by the statute of limitations and had no chance of succeeding in a court of law? Boies was a good enough lawyer to understand this. What, then, was his game plan when he spent hours meeting with Wexner's lawyers and describing in detail the accusations Giuffre was leveling against this multibillionaire? Moreover, why did Giuffre's legal team accuse me in public court filings but make no mention of Wexner? Why did they decide to approach Wexner privately to discuss Giuffre's allegations against him but to name Prince Andrew and me publicly? Was it true what Rebecca Boylan said that Giuffre had told her: that she was seeking a megabuck payday from Wexner despite the fact that the statute of limitations barred any lawsuit?

I don't know whether Virginia Giuffre's accusation that Leslie Wexner had had sex with her on multiple occasions when she was underage is true or false, though I suspect it is false. Nor do I know whether her accusations against the other prominent and wealthy friends and associates of Epstein are true or false. All I know for certain is that she is lying about me and has a long, sordid history of lying about other prominent men. I do not know whether David Boies believes her accusations against Wexner to be true or false. But if Boies believes them to be true, then why wasn't Wexner accused in public like I was? Why was he accused only in private? Why has he not been sued under the new statute of limitations that permits underage victims to sue for criminal acts that took place decades ago? If Boies believes that Giuffre's very specific accusations against Wexner are false—as his co-counsel Bradley Edwards has acknowledged[38]—how can he continue to maintain that her nearly identical allegations against me are true? How can he continue to represent someone who he believes made up a story about Wexner in an effort to obtain a billion dollars from him? Why is he continuing to vouch for her credibility if he knows she lied about Wexner and others?

I leave it to the reader to answer these questions—or for Boies to provide an explanation.

Thus far, Boies, who has been outspoken on many other issues, has refused to address these difficult questions about Wexner. Because one possible answer to these questions may suggest a criminal "shakedown" of Wexner, I took the matter to both federal and state prosecutors. I showed them the evidence, played the tapes and laid out the possible criminal scenarios. I relate what occurred in Chapter 11.

---

38 See Chapter 9.

CHAPTER 6

Being Exculpated

Prior to the advent of the #MeToo movement in the fall of 2017, my case was closed. The judge had struck the false accusation as irrelevant and impertinent and had sanctioned the lawyers who had filed it. An independent investigation by the former Director of the FBI, Louis Freeh, had concluded that the accusation was disproved. Here is the text of Freeh's conclusion:

> Over the past several months, an independent investigation was conducted, under my supervision by former senior federal law enforcement officials. We interviewed many witnesses and reviewed thousands of pages of documentary evidence. Our investigation found no evidence to support the accusation of sexual misconduct against professor Dershowitz. In fact, in several instances, the evidence directly contradicted the accusations made against him.
>
> In my opinion, the totality of the evidence found during the investigation refutes the allegations made against Professor Dershowitz. (Appendix I)

On March 9, 2019, the Chief Executive Officer of the Freeh Group issued a supplementary statement detailing aspects of the investigation. It included the following:

During the course of our investigation, personnel from FGIS, including a former senior prosecutor and investigator from the U.S. Department of Justice with more than a half century of collective experience conducing criminal investigations, carefully examined thousands of pages of documentary evidence, much of which Professor Dershowitz supplied to us; sought to reconstruct events in New York City, Palm Beach, Little St. James Island, a ranch in New Mexico, and on a private aircraft; and identified and interviewed many witnesses who were able to provide relevant details regarding Ms. Roberts' allegations. In our opinion, the totality of the evidence found during the investigation refutes the allegations made against Professor Dershowitz.

In addition, FCIS made a Freedom of Information Act ("FOIA") request to the U.S. Secret Service ("USSS") for "any and all sift logs, travel records, itineraries, reports and other records for USSS personnel traveling with former President William Clinton to Little St. James Island." This was done in an effort to determine whether former President Clinton had been there as Ms. Roberts alleged.

On January 16, 2016, the official in charge of the USSS's FIOA/PA Office replied by letter that the "USSS has conducted a reasonable search for responsive records" and "from a review of USSS main indices, that there are no records pertaining to your request that are referenced in these indices." Thus, the conclusion that can be drawn that, contrary to Ms. Roberts' allegation, Former President Clinton did not in fact travel to, nor was he present on, Little St. James Island between January 1, 2002 and January 1, 2003. The FOIA results not only directly impeach Ms. Roberts' specific allegations against Professor Dershowitz, but in our opinion completely undermine her credibility. Together with our other factual findings and conclusions, it is our opinion that all of these allegations against him were made without any basis.

At the conclusion of our investigation, which was conducted under the supervision of FGIS Chairman, Louis J. Freeh, FGIS concluded that we "found no evidence to support the accusation of sexual misconduct against Professor Dershowitz. In fact, in several instances, the evidence directly contradicted the accusations made against him."

We stand by our investigation and that conclusion.

(See Appendix I)

My accuser's own lawyer had told me—on tape—he had reviewed my travel and other records and had come to the conclusion that it would have been "impossible" for me to have been in locations where Giuffre claimed to have sex with me and that she was "wrong . . . simply wrong" in accusing me. The text of this admission is set out in Chapter 4. Finally, the lawyers who filed the pleadings accusing me of sexual misconduct acknowledged that it was a mistake to have done so and formally withdrew them. This is what Giuffre's lawyers agreed to say in a statement approved by all parties, with regard to Giuffre's accusation:

> Dershowitz completely denies any such misconduct, while not disputing Robert's statements that the underlying alleged misconduct may have occurred with someone else. Dershowitz has produced travel and other records for the relevant times which he relies on to establish that he could not have been present when the alleged misconduct occurred. He has also produced other evidence that he relies upon to refute the credibility of the allegations against him.
>
> The parties believe it is time *to take advantage of the new information* that has come to light on both sides during the litigation and put these matters behind them.
>
> Given the events that have transpired since the filing of the documents in the federal court and in this action in which Dershowitz was accused of sexual misconduct, including the court order striking the allegations in the federal court filings, and the records and other documents produced by the parties, *Edwards and Cassell acknowledge that it was a mistake to have filed sexual misconduct accusations against Dershowitz*; and the sexual misconduct accusations made in all public filings (including all exhibits) are thereby withdrawn. (emphasis added)

They later argued that the "mistake" to which they admitted was merely "tactical," not substantive, but that's not what their binding statement says, nor is it what was agreed to. Indeed, the explicit reference to my "travel and other records for the relevant times" and to "the new information" make it clear that their mistake was substantive: they should not have falsely accused an innocent man of sexual misconduct. That is the far more reasonable interpretation of their statement.

It was a costly mistake for me because the false accusation—the recent fabrication—was published and transmitted all around the world. And false accusations can't simply be struck, withdrawn, or called a mistake. The original story, containing the false accusation, received far more attention than the subsequent stories about the evidence that proved my innocence and the withdrawal of the false accusation.

The accusations against me were no longer in the news, but the stench lingered. Lawyers like to point out that when prejudicial evidence is presented to a jury and then struck by the judge, it's like "throwing a skunk into the jury box: when the skunk is removed the smell remains."

It is impossible to describe what it feels like to be accused of a terrible crime with which you had absolutely nothing to do. It's not like some white-collar crimes, such as fraud, which are often matters of degree. Nor is it like an accusation of an acquaintance rape, in which sex occurred and there is a dispute over whether it was consensual. In my case, there was no matter of degree, no gray area. It was a completely made-up story, motivated by money. I often wonder what it must feel like to the woman who willfully accuses an innocent person of a heinous sexual crime that she knows he didn't commit. It's hard to imagine any decent woman—even if she herself had been abused—putting an innocent person through such a horrible experience.

Yet, despite the absence of any evidence that I did anything wrong, in the court of public opinion—as distinguished from the court of law—the burden of proof was on me to prove that I had never met her. And it was a heavy burden. I had to prove a negative—and I had to prove it conclusively. Beyond a reasonable doubt would not be enough. There could be no lingering doubt—reasonable or unreasonable.

I was prepared to meet that burden despite the fact that my accuser refused to provide any time frame for her accusations, beyond the two-year period she knew Jeffrey Epstein. But she deliberately lied even about *that* broad time frame. Originally, she claimed that she had met Jeffrey Epstein in June of 1998, when she was fourteen, distinctly recalling spending her "sweet sixteen" birthday with Epstein. She said she met Epstein's friend Ghislaine Maxwell while she was working at Donald Trump's Mar-a-Lago resort in Palm Beach and that she got the job there after her father had worked there for a while. But the employment records of Mar-a-Lago proved conclusively that her father did not begin to work there until Giuffre was nearly seventeen,[39] and that she almost certainly met Jeffrey Epstein when she was well past seventeen, not fourteen as she had falsely claimed. According to her own account, she did not begin to have sex with any of Epstein's associates until about two years after meeting Epstein[40]—which would have put her well above eighteen when she claimed to have had her first sexual encounter with an Epstein acquaintance, and close to 19 when she had subsequent encounters.

The reason she lied so dramatically about her age is because the age of consent is seventeen in most of the places she claimed to have had sex with Jeffrey Epstein's friends. If she was over seventeen and was paid to have sex—she says she was paid fifteen thousand dollars to have sex with Prince Andrew—it was she who was committing a crime. Her age was, of course, irrelevant to me, since I *never* had sex with her at *any* age. But it proves that she deliberately lied about her age, as she did about meeting Al Gore, Tipper Gore, and Bill Clinton.

Even after it was proved conclusively that she had committed

---

39 The records show that he began to work there on April 11, 2000. We have been advised that the spa where Giuffre worked closes between Mother's Day and late summer. If that is the case, then the earliest Giuffre could have begun working there is October 2000, when she was over 17.

40 See Sharon Churcher, Virginia Roberts' account of the explosive Prince Andrew 'Sex Slave' Drama, *Daily Mail*, Jan. 4, 2015.

numerous acts of perjury, she remained a free woman, unpunished for repeatedly lying under oath and deliberately seeking to destroy the reputation of an innocent victim of a financially motivated frame-up. Nor was I the only victim of her perjury. Every real victim of sexual assault suffers when a false "victim" is caught in a lie, as Giuffre has been.

In a court filing I issued the following invitation to prosecutors:

> *I never had sexual contact with Ms. Giuffre of any kind. . . . By swearing to this, I am deliberately exposing myself to a perjury prosecution and disbarment if I am not telling the truth. If Ms. Giuffre were to submit an affidavit repeating her false allegations against me [which she did], I would welcome and cooperate with a criminal investigation by any prosecutorial office as to whether it is Ms. Giuffre or I who is committing perjury. It is inescapably clear that one of us is lying under oath. I know it is not me.*

I believe failing to prosecute perjury by adult women—she was over thirty when she first committed perjury about me and she is 36 now—who falsely and willfully accuse men of heinous sex crimes for money constitutes an unacceptable double standard in a society seeking to move toward gender equality under the law. I am committed to seeing the law changed so that no other innocent person should have to endure being falsely accused of a crime without having recourse under the rule of law. Currently, lawyers, clients, and witnesses can make defamatory statements in public court filings and depositions without fear of a civil suit or a perjury prosecution. As Judge Cabranes put it in a recent decision: "It is in fact exceedingly rare for anyone to be prosecuted for perjury in a civil proceeding." It is these realities that incentivized Giuffre and her lawyers to falsely accuse me of a crime with complete impunity: they believed that I could not sue them, because their allegations were contained in a court filing, and were thus immune from a defamation suit. Even more absurdly, by denying Giuffre's allegations and saying they were lies, I subjected myself to a defamation suit. (More on this later.)

Having won my case in the court of public opinion—at least until the #MeToo movement resuscitated it—I drew some lessons and proposed some remedies:

"Academics have long complained that the absolute litigation privilege puts victims of defamation in an unfair position. Courts have generally responded that the truth-finding mission of judicial proceedings outweighs any individual interest in reputational integrity.
So what is to be done?
There are two principal avenues through which the Kafkaesque situation in which I found myself could be avoided in the future. Lawyers should be disciplined for filing false allegations without performing adequate due diligence. Victims of a defamatory accusation made within the scope of the litigation privilege must be allowed to deny the accusation in the strongest terms without fear of a defamation suit. Under current law, the marketplace of ideas is skewed in favor of the false accuser and against the falsely accused victim. Courts must level the playing field between accused and accuser by granting reciprocal immunity from defamation to persons being falsely accused, so that they are able to fully defend themselves in the court of public opinion.
There are no perfect solutions in a nation rightly committed both to the role of courts in resolving disputes and to the protection of free expression. Ultimately, the responsibility lies with decent lawyers to refuse to level unfounded allegations against innocent individuals. I leave it to the reader to decide whether Virginia Roberts Giuffre's lawyers satisfied this responsibility."[41]

My proposals stimulated some debate, but then along came the #MeToo movement, which stifled debate, shifted the presumption from innocence to guilt, and made it nearly impossible for a man falsely accused of a sex crime to prove his innocence, regardless of the evidence or lack thereof.

---

41 Alan Dershowitz, *Taking the Stand*, 400-401 (Paperback edition, 2019).

CHAPTER 7

The #MeToo Movement: Virtues, Vices and Suggested Improvements

The #MeToo movement began with a series of media exposés of Harvey Weinstein. I had represented Weinstein's company with regard to First Amendment issues in his early years as a film producer. I helped his films secure appropriate ratings from the Motion Picture Association of America. When he was recently indicted, his lawyers sought my legal advice about obtaining exculpatory emails from his accusers. I had been litigating to obtain the exculpatory emails in my own case, so I shared my experience and expertise with his lawyers. (Ironically, David Boies had been Weinstein's original lawyer trying to stop the media from reporting about this alleged harassment, but when *The New York Times*—whom he had also been representing—discovered that Boies had hired an investigative firm to intimidate *Times* reporters who were covering Weinstein, the *Times* fired him and he stopped representing Weinstein.)

The Weinstein exposé led other women to come forward against prominent men, and the #MeToo movement was born. The philosopher Eric Hoffer once described the evolution—or devolution—of movements as follows: "Every great cause begins as a movement, becomes a business, and eventually degenerates into a racket."[42] Only time will tell whether this becomes the fate of #MeToo. One thing is already clear: some unscrupulous lawyers are trying to exploit the #MeToo movement for personal profit by helping women file false or exaggerated accusations against innocent men. If this tactic is allowed to succeed—if there are no consequences for levelling knowingly false accusations—it will spread and become a "racket."

A corollary to Hoffer's cynical, if prescient, assessment is the historical truth that some movements and causes are driven by an "ends justify the means" mentality. Some zealots who push these movements and causes are so convinced of their righteousness that they become intolerant of dissent, due process and other cumbersome barriers to their truth, with a capital T—a Truth of which they are absolutely certain. For them, procedural safeguards—such as the presumption of innocence and the requirement that the accuser prove her case by evidence—are unnecessary when a woman accuses a man of sexual assault. But as Justice Felix Frankfurter once reminded us: "The history of liberty has largely been the history of observance of procedural safeguards."[43]

We are already seeing the decreasing respect for such safeguards with the #MeToo movement. For some in that movement, an accusation by a woman is enough to establish guilt, because "women don't lie," and "women must be believed," about being sexually assaulted.

The point these advocates are making is that women who said they were sexually assaulted have been routinely disbelieved over the years, and the time has come—indeed, it is long overdue—when the presumption should shift from disbelief to belief. There is much to be said for this view, but it must not deny the falsely accused the right to prove his innocence. There is no gender-linked gene for truth telling or lying.

Consider, for example, Meghan McCain's demand that I be banned from TV because I was "accused" by Giuffre. I will discuss

---

42   He also put it this way: "What started out here as a mass movement ends up as a racket, a cult, or a corporation." *The Temper of Our Times.*

43   McNabb v. United States, 318 U.S. 332, 347 (1943).

this demand at greater length in Chapter 10, but for now it is enough to note that *both* Giuffre and I have been accused of serious crimes: I was accused by Giuffre of having sex with her, and she is accused by me of committing perjury in falsely accusing me. My evidence is far stronger than hers—indeed, she has *no* evidence. Yet, McCain would not demand that *she* be banned from TV because she has been accused. To the contrary, she would be welcomed by McCain on her show, as she has been on others.

Moreover, women victims may be telling the truth about some aspects of their victimization and lying about other aspects. That may well be the situation with Giuffre. A person who, at a young age, has been repeatedly abused—as Giuffre apparently had been even before she met Epstein—may develop coping mechanisms for surviving abuse. These mechanisms may include lying and stealing[44]—both of which Giuffre has been caught doing. This doesn't mean she wasn't herself a victim of someone's abuse, but it may mean that she has victimized others as well through her abusive dishonesty.

* * *

Giuffre may well be telling the truth about having been victimized by Epstein, but she is lying about me. I don't know whether she is telling the truth or lying about others, but there is a Latin legal principle that says *"falsus in uno, falsus in omnibus"*—"False in one thing, false in everything." This may well overstate the reality, because some people can be telling the truth about certain matters, while lying about others. But judges do and should instruct juries to view with "skepticism"—some say distrust—the testimony of witnesses who have a proven record of lying. The same should be true in the court of public opinion.

In general, the testimony of one witness is sufficient to make a legal case, even if it is uncorroborated. But when that witness has a history of lying—especially about related issues or people—some

---

44 According to a police report, Giuffre was fired from a restaurant job for stealing money.

degree of corroboration should be demanded before their accusations are credited, especially if serious consequences flow from believing him or her. That makes common sense and is consistent with fairness and due process.

Yet in the era of #MeToo, that common-sense approach is often not followed when it comes to accusations of sexual misconduct by a woman against a man. In my case, Giuffre has falsely accused other prominent men for money. She has lied about how old she was when she met Epstein. She was caught stealing money from a business where she had worked. She is lying about her non-fiction manuscript being a novel. Yet her uncorroborated accusation against me has been credited by some in the #MeToo movement and the media despite the overwhelming evidence that she is lying.

The #MeToo movement must not become hostage to those who seek to exploit it and turn it into a racket. It must distinguish between true victims of sex abuse, false victims and those who may have elements of both. It must become more nuanced in its assessment of accusations. If the mantra that *all* women *always* tell the truth and that *all* women should *always* be believed were to become widely accepted, it would simply substitute one form of sexism for another. In the past, too many women were *disbelieved* just because they were women. The #MeToo movement rightfully challenged that over-general stereotype. But the other over-general stereotype—that *no* woman should *ever* be disbelieved—must be challenged as well. The #MeToo movement began as an understandable reaction against the sexism of allowing predatory men to get away with abusing women. It should not be allowed to be distorted into an overreaction that allows greedy women and their lawyers to turn innocent men into victims of deliberately false accusations.

Despite the sordid history of women not being believed, there is no place for "affirmative action" when accusations of sexual abuse are disputed. Women and men should be treated equally when it comes to credibility. The presumption of innocence should be applied to both genders and the burden of proof should fall on accusers, regardless of their gender. The burden should, of course, be higher in criminal than in civil cases, but no one should be presumed guilty or liable without convincing evidence. The noble *ends* of gender equality must not be allowed to justify the elimination of due process as a reliable *means* for assessing serious accusations of sexual misconduct.

David Boies and his legal team have not only hurt the #MeToo movement, they have hurt their own client by having her submit perjured affidavits about me. She may well be telling the truth about Epstein and others, but her general credibility as witness has been shattered by her proven lies about me.

Ironically, Boies told me that he thought it was a mistake to have Giuffre accuse me and that her account regarding Epstein and others would have been far more credible had she not included me. (Appendix B) Boies knows that I never met Giuffre and has admitted—in a recorded conversation—that she was "simply wrong" in accusing me, because it would have been "impossible" for me to have been in the places she claims to have met me.

Giuffre's provably false sworn statements make it impossible for ethical government lawyers—or for any ethical lawyers—now to vouch for her credibility. Had she not falsely accused me, her credibility might be intact. For reporters to rely on the credibility of witnesses with a proven record of perjury—as the *Miami Herald*, *The New Yorker*, NBC's *Dateline* and others have done—diminishes the general credibility of their reporting. (See Chapter 10) False witnesses also hurt the #MeToo movement by casting doubt on the credibility of truthful victims. Boies is not a hero of the #MeToo movement, despite his crass efforts to anoint himself as such. He is a villain who has hurt innocent people, damaged a positive movement and, most shamefully, diminished the credibility of his own clients—all for self-serving and self-enriching purposes.

There is an important difference between a *criminal* defense lawyer who *must* defend his client even if he knows his client is guilty, and a *civil* plaintiff's lawyer who *must never* bring a lawsuit charging a defendant with serious misconduct if he knows the defendant is innocent. Even a criminal defense lawyer may not call the defendant or any other witness to the stand if the lawyer knows the witness will lie.

The noble ends of the #MeToo movement do not justify the ignoble means of allowing a client to falsely accuse an innocent man.

The #MeToo movement will be judged by history and not just by the passions of the moment. For it to be remembered as a positive movement, rather than as a business and racket, it must not allow those who would wrongly exploit it for personal profit to hide behind its virtuous shield, turning it into an exploitative sword against innocent people.

CHAPTER 8

A Pattern of Perjury Suborned

In sexual assault cases, prosecutors often seek to introduce evidence that the accused rapist had a pattern of prior assaults that gives credence to the accusation for which he is standing trial. Such a pattern can constitute powerful corroboration for an alleged victim's testimony. In Bill Cosby's first trial, prosecutors failed to introduce pattern evidence and the result was a hung jury. In the second trial, they introduced the testimony of other women who said they were drugged before being raped. The jury then convicted.[45] In the Weinstein case, the prosecutor—over strong objection by the defense—is being permitted to introduce pattern evidence.

But there is another side of the coin with regard to pattern evidence. Sometimes there is a pattern of perjury or of suborning perjury for financial gain. In my case, after I proved that Giuffre was lying, her lawyers got two other women to follow her pattern.[46]

David Boies had threatened to find "another girl" to accuse me, unless I withdrew disciplinary charges I had filed against him with bar associations. As he told my source, "Two are better than one."

45 Kris Maher, Bill Consby Is Found Guilty in Second Trial for Sexual Assault, *Wall Street Journal*, April. 26, 2018..

46 Stephen Rex Brown, Second Woman Claims Billionaire Perv Jeffrey Epstein 'Directed' Her to Have Sex with Alan Dershowitz, *New York Daily News*, Dec. 18, 2018; Julie K. Brown, New Jeffrey Epstein Accuser Emerges; Defamation Suit Filed, *Miami Herald*, April 16, 2019.

That person told me that Boies was "trolling" for another woman to accuse me. I refused to withdraw the charges, and he "found" a thirty-something-year-old woman named Sarah Ransome, who was willing to say that she had participated in a "threesome" with me when she was 22 years old and working with Epstein. As with Giuffre, I had never met or heard of this liar. She, too, had made up the story *after* meeting with and presumably being pressured by the same lawyer or lawyers who had pressured Giuffre to lie about me. The pattern was beginning to become obvious. But this woman was even a bigger liar—which she eventually *admitted*—than Giuffre. In the run-up to the 2016 presidential election, Ransome wrote dozens of emails to a reporter for the *New York Post* claiming that she possessed "sex tapes" of Hillary Clinton, Donald Trump, Bill Clinton and Richard Branson. (Appendix H)

She also claimed to have been targeted for assassination by Hillary Clinton and the CIA and that she was working with Russian KGB to prevent the election of the two "pedophiles" who were running for president. The *New York Post* reporter asked her for proof of what she was saying, but the woman had none. So the reporter told me that she concluded that Ransome was either hallucinating or lying and refused to publish her claims even on the gossipy Page 6. But what wasn't credible enough for Page 6 was apparently credible enough for David Boies, who vouched for Ransome's truthfulness by filing her affidavit falsely accusing me.

It is a sad sign of the times that the *New York Post* reporter has refused to publish these emails—which she and the *Post* are free to do. They, like other media, refuse to disclose negative factual information about alleged #MeToo victims, if such information would undercut the politically correct, but often factually incorrect, narrative of victimization.

In her emails, Ransome, like Giuffre, mentioned me. And like Giuffre, she mentioned me as someone *she did not* have sex with. She claimed, quite absurdly, that I had been her lawyer and was suing a man who met her on the "sugar daddy" website where young women express a willingness to exchange sex with wealthy men for money. Of course she had no evidence—no retainer agreement, court documents, letters, witnesses or anything else—to support her absurd claim, because I had never met her and was not her lawyer. But that isn't the important point. What is critical is that the story she made up about me *before* meeting her lawyers was that I was her lawyer and *not* her sex partner. She concocted the phony sex story about me only *after* she met her greedy lawyers, who were aware that she had previously made up false stories about the sex tapes and Clinton assassination plot.[47]

When I publicized Ransome's many lies, she was forced to admit to a journalist that she had "invented" the story and the sex tapes in order to take revenge against Epstein and prevent him from harming her.[48] She did not say why she invented the story about me, but the obvious reason is that it was part of a pattern of being pressured by the same lawyer or lawyers who had pressured Giuffre into falsely accusing me.

Perhaps two nearly identical instances of lying as a result of being pressured by the same lawyers does not constitute a pattern, but three does. And there is indeed a third component of the pattern.

A woman named Maria Farmer worked for Epstein in his New York home until the early summer of 1996, when she claims he assaulted her on Leslie Wexner's property in New Albany, Ohio. She

47 The actual emails—dozens of them—remain sealed, but the *Post* reporter told me their content and I'm free to repeat what she told me and I memorialized in a contemporaneous memorandum. See Appendix H. Eventually, Ransome's mendacious emails will be unsealed, and I will send them to appropriate bar associations and prosecutors to assess the conduct of lawyers who would submit affidavits from so obviously non-credible an accuser.

48 As Connie Bruck reported in her long *New Yorker* profile, "For Ransome, as for the other women, these benefits [from Epstein] depended on her having sex with Epstein and with his friends. In her affidavit, she named Dershowitz as one of those friends. Ransome was another imperfect witness. In the fall of 2016, she had suggested to the *New York Post* that she had sex tapes of half a dozen prominent people, including Bill Clinton and Donald Trump – but couldn't provide the tapes when asked. (Ransome told me that she invented the tapes to draw attention to Epstein's behavior, and to make him believe that she had "evidence that would come out if he harmed me.")" Connie Bruck, Alan Dershowitz, Devil's Advocate, *The New Yorker*, July 29, 2019.
 Bruck was misstating the facts when she "reported" that Ransome had merely "suggested" that she had sex tapes of Bill Clinton and Donald Trump. She had *categorically stated* that she had actual possession of such tapes. Bruck also conveniently left out Hillary Clinton from the list of sex tapes that Ransome claimed to have.

then stopped working for Epstein and never again set foot in his house. Boies—who else?—submitted an affidavit from Farmer swearing she had seen me in Epstein's house *when she worked for him.* She swore she saw me in the presence of young women, though she said she didn't witness any wrongdoing on my part.[49] The problem with her affidavit is that I didn't even meet Epstein until *well after* she stopped working for him, and was never in his house until months after she stopped coming there. The documented chronology makes it impossible for her to have seen me in his house. Yet Boies submitted her perjured affidavit, knowing that I hadn't even met Epstein, and was certainly never in his house, until *after* she terminated her relationship with him.

Thus, the pattern of perjury is clear: three women, all represented by the same lawyers, *change* their stories in an effort to incriminate me only *after* meeting these lawyers and apparently being pressured by them.

I believe this insidious pattern should be investigated by law enforcement. Subornation of perjury is a serious crime,[50] especially when committed by lawyers. A pattern of subornation is even more serious. If such a pattern in fact occurred with three perjuring women, and if their perjury was suborned by lawyers, there should be legal consequences.

In any event, none of these three women should now be believed, based on the indisputable evidence that they are lying. Three false witnesses are not better than one, especially if all three are represented and pressured by the same lawyers. Some may say that where there's smoke, there must be fire. But is some cases, like this one, the smoke may be a sign of arson—of three fires set by the same team of arsonists.

---

49   https://www.scribd.com/document/406613394/Affidavit-of-Maria-Farmer.
50   Title 18 U.S.C. § 1622.

CHAPTER 9

A Mystery Following Epstein's Suicide: Why Did David Boies Drop the Ball against Leslie Wexner?

When I was informed that my former client Jeffrey Epstein may have tried to kill himself in jail, I was not surprised. Based on the evidence in the case, it seems apparent that Epstein was a hedonist who cared about his body, his comforts, his pleasures and his well-being. I never saw him drink or use drugs. He ate very little. He worked out. His pleasures obviously focused on sex.

I was surprised that Epstein flew into Teterboro airport while an investigation of him was ongoing. He could easily have remained in Paris where he owned an apartment. I had never seen his Paris condo, but I'm told it was quite beautiful. Had he stayed in France, the US would have sought to extradite him, but it is uncertain whether they would have succeeded. Recall that Roman Polanski, whom I had briefly represented, lived openly in France despite American efforts to extradite him when he fled California following his guilty plea for having sex with an underage girl.

* * *

Epstein was probably unaware of the investigation and indictment by the US Attorney's office in Manhattan. He must have been shocked to be arrested. He must have been even more shocked to see the inside of the federal detention center that would be his new home. I have been in that facility to visit clients, and it is hell on earth even for inmates who are not used to living in the palatial homes that Epstein owned.

When the government opposed his pretrial release, Epstein probably realized that he might never again experience freedom. Prosecutors win the vast majority of their cases and motions, and if convicted he was facing a sentence that would likely keep him imprisoned for the rest of his life. I suspect that he did not see any light at the end of the tunnel, and did not want to spend the next several decades as a federal prisoner. So suicide was an obvious option.

Though I was not surprised when Epstein *attempted* suicide, I was shocked when, a few weeks later, he *succeeded*. It is nearly impossible for a prisoner on suicide watch to kill himself. Such prisoners are denied access to any material they could use to hang themselves—belts, shoelaces, sheets etc. They are continuously monitored by guards and video cameras. But Epstein was not only taken off suicide watch, his cell mate was moved and he was left alone and unmonitored with his bedsheets. It is almost as if they were inviting him to hang himself, which he did.

The autopsy confirmed suicide, but there are skeptics, including some of his current lawyers, who were preparing to appeal the denial of bail and to defend him vigorously at trial. There will be investigations, but I doubt there will be hard evidence that he may have been killed by others.

Epstein's death caused understandable anger among his victims and alleged victims. The judge who was supposed to preside over his criminal case invited his alleged victims—including my false accusers Giuffre and Ransome—to speak in court. Neither mentioned me. On the courthouse steps, Giuffre demanded that Prince Andrew come clean, yet she didn't dare accuse me because she knew I would sue her if she repeated out of court the perjurious lies she had told in court papers.

Epstein's death left many unsolved mysteries which should be investigated. At the center of these mysteries is Leslie Wexner.

Wexner's *business* relationships with Epstein have received considerable attention, but there has been little coverage of their long term *personal* relationships and the accusations made by Giuffre that Wexner had sex with her, and perhaps others.[51]

A deep mystery surrounds the decision by attorney David Boies not to pursue Wexner, to whom, according to Giuffre, she was sexually trafficked by Jeffrey Epstein on multiple occasions while she was underage.[52] Readers may be unaware of these allegations because Boies deep-sixed them after meeting with Wexner's lawyer. The question is, why? Did Boies not believe his client's accusations against Wexner? If he did believe them, did Wexner pay hush money to keep the accusations from becoming public? The answer may lie in the following documented, but suppressed, story that I have asked prosecutors to investigate.

In mid-2014, Giuffre's original lawyer, a former Assistant Attorney General named Stanley Pottinger, asked Boies to help represent Giuffre. Boies agreed. According to a sworn affidavit filed by Pottinger:

> In the fall of 2014, I asked Mr. Boies if the firm represented, or if he knew, Mr. Leslie Wexner. I told him that in the course of investigating facts related to Mr. Epstein's sex trafficking, Mr. Wexner had been identified as a close business associate and personal friend of Mr. Epstein. I told Mr. Boies that there were assertions that Mr. Wexner had permitted Mr. Epstein to use, and entertain on, Mr. Wexner's yacht, *and that Mr. Wexner was alleged to have had sex with one or more of Mr. Epstein's girls, including Ms. Giuffre.* (emphasis added)

The Pottinger affidavit disclosed that in December of 2014—precisely the same time I was being *publicly* accused in court papers by Giuffre of having had sex with her—Boies's firm asked to meet with Wexner *privately*. As previously noted, Boies and his partner then met with

51 See excerpts from Pottinger Affidavit in Appendix J.
52 See *supra* pages 75-76.

Wexner's lawyer and told him, according to the lawyer, that Giuffre was accusing him of sexual misconduct similar to that of which she was falsely accusing me. As I've said, both Wexner's wife and his lawyer used the word "shakedown" when telling me about Boies's approach to Wexner. They also said the accusations were untrue. We don't know precisely what transpired at the secret meeting, but we do know, from the records of the case, that following the meeting, Wexner's name disappeared from court filings, and no public accusation, of the kind made against me, was ever leveled against Wexner by Boies or his client. In the recently unsealed deposition of Giuffre taken in 2016, she accuses many prominent figures of having sex with her, but *not* Wexner, though she had earlier accused him in secret.

Wexner's disappearance from the Epstein cases is surprising, indeed shocking, in light of Wexner's wealth and long-term personal and business associations with Epstein. Maria Farmer—whose credibility is questionable—has sworn that she was assaulted by Epstein on Wexner's property, after Wexner hired her to work with him, and that "Wexner's security staff refused to let [her] leave the property," where she was "held against [her] will for 12 hours . . ."

As I have repeatedly said, the accusations against me, which were deliberately made public, are refuted by the evidence. Yet they were deliberately made in *publicly* filed court documents and then leaked to the press in order to gain maximum publicity. Just as these accusations became headline news, Wexner was approached *privately* with similar accusations. The timing does not appear to be coincidental.

It would be commendable, if Boies had indeed met with Wexner's lawyers in order to "thoroughly investigate" the accusations, as the Pottinger affidavit claims. If Wexner's lawyers persuaded Boies that his client was lying about having sex with Wexner, that would be a good explanation for why they would not, thereafter, have publicly accused Wexner. But it doesn't explain why they continued to publicly accuse *me* after concluding that the very woman who accused me—the *same* one who accused Wexner—was a liar, who made up a *similar* false story about another prominent man.

If, on the other hand, Boies believed that Giuffre was telling the truth about Wexner, why would he possibly have allowed this prominent multi-billionaire to get away with having repeatedly abused his "underage" client? Boies sued Ghislaine Maxwell and Epstein on behalf of his clients and received generous settlements from which he received contingency fees. Now Giuffre is suing me, as I will describe in the Chapter 12. Why did he let the mega-wealthiest person most closely connected to Epstein off the hook? Did money change hands?

There is no third possibility: Either Boies concluded that Giuffre was lying about Wexner, in which case she should not be believed about me; or he concluded that she was telling the truth about Wexner, in which case, Boies has to explain why he covered up this billionaire's serious crimes against his client.

It is, of course, *logically possible* that Giuffre was lying about Wexner (as well as the Gores, Clinton, her age and other issues) but telling the truth about me. But as Oliver Wendell Holmes wisely observed, "The Life of the law has not been logic, it has been experience."[53] And experience teaches that a witness who has falsely accused others and lied about relevant matters should not be believed. Giuffre's own lawyer, David Boies, acknowledged this when he told me that she was "wrong" about meeting me on the island, ranch and other locations so she could not be believed about meeting me in New York.

Not only did Leslie Wexner's name completely disappear from the case after his lawyer met with Boies and McCawley, but Giuffre's lawyers went out of their way to pronounce him innocent of any wrongdoing. Here is how Bradly Edwards, Giuffre's Florida lawyer, put it when asked on July 16, 2019 whether Wexner was involved with any of Jeffrey Epstein's sexual misconduct:

"I believe based on the information that we have accumulated over 11 years that the statements that he gave yesterday in the press that he did not know about the sexual proclivities of Mr. Epstein are very likely to be true. We have not seen where he is in the company of Jeffrey Epstein at the time he when was engaging in these things. In fact, it is very seldom that any of the victims ever met him or saw him, I know there are a lot of business ties to him but other than

---

53   Oliver Wendell Holmes, *The Common Law* (1881).

receiving any information about their business connection, I don't
have any information to believe otherwise."

This interview is highly significant, because Edwards was speaking as
Giuffre's *lawyer* and *agent*. In doing so, he was admitting—much like
Boies has previously admitted—that his own client was a liar and a
perjurer. Recall that Giuffre had testified under oath that she had sex
with Wexner on numerous occasions, under circumstances nearly
identical to the false claims she made about having had sex with me.
She has also accused Wexner of making her wear Victoria's Secret-
type lingerie while he had sex with her. Giuffre also told another of
her lawyers, Pottinger, that Wexner had sex with her and may have
had sex with other women associated with Epstein. But that was all
before Boies and McCawley met with Wexner's lawyers. If, in fact,
Wexner paid hush money to buy Giuffre's silence, then it would be
understandable why Edwards was prepared to deny that she had sex
with Wexner. But this has the effect of throwing his client under the
bus by, in effect, calling her a perjurer for swearing that she did have
sex with Wexner.

If Edwards made this dramatic and damming admission because
he knows that Giuffre lied about Wexner, then he surely should not
have believed her nearly identical false claims about me. This is a
deep conundrum for the Giuffre team, and one that may well suggest
serious criminal conduct.

And there is more. In a previous interview Edwards said that
based on his own 11 years of investigating Epstein related charges he
doesn't "know of any high profile people who would be implicated"
in sexual misconduct. So, again, he is calling his client a perjurer because she testified that among the people she was forced by Epstein to
have sex with there were many extremely "high profile people" such
as George Mitchell, Bill Richardson, Ehud Barak and others.

It is, of course, possible that Giuffre's lawyers are seeking hush money from these and other prominent figures who have been accused by
Giuffre, whether falsely or truthfully. Anyone who doubts that Boies
and his firm are capable of such tactics need only look at the case of
Emma Cline, a young novelist who received the Boies treatment.

Boies and his firm represented the ex-boyfriend of writer Emma Cline, who wrote the acclaimed novel *Girls*, a fictional account of a woman's relationship with Charles Manson. The ex-boyfriend, Chaz Reetz-Laiolo, alleged that she stole his writing for her book and invaded his privacy via a spyware program named Refog installed on her laptop. Reetz-Laiolo had use of her computer during their relationship, and later bought it from Cline after their romance ended.

In an effort to "settle" the case, Boies and his team sent Cline and her lawyers a draft complaint—with Boies' name—that sought to stop the sale of *Girls* and a movie deal based on the book.

The draft complaint came with a not-so-veiled-threat of what would happen if no settlement was reached. As *The New Yorker* reported,

"Boies Schiller responded by sending a hundred-and-ten-page draft of a complaint that it said it was prepared to file in court if the two sides did not reach a settlement. David Boies's name appeared at the top of it. Reading through the allegations, Cline was stunned to find a section titled "Cline's History of Manipulating Older Men," which purported to illustrate how Boies Schiller would easily discredit her arguments about her former boyfriend's treatment of her before a jury. "[E]vidence shows that Cline was not the innocent and inexperienced naïf she portrayed herself to be, and had instead for many years maintained numerous 'relations' with older men and others, from whom she extracted gifts and money," the section began. What followed were thirteen pages containing screenshots of explicit chat conversations with lovers, including one in which Cline had sent a naked photo of herself (the photo was blacked out in the letter) to a boyfriend, explicit banter with people she'd met online, and snippets of her most intimate diary entries. All of this material had been recorded by the spyware and remained on Cline's old laptop, which Reetz-Laiolo now had in his possession."

Cline's lawyers disclosed the draft complaint with these salacious materials.

In their counter complaint[54], Cline's lawyers minced no words in
describing Boies Schiller's tactics.

> His [Reetz-Laiolo'] allegations follow a pattern that started during
> their relationship – and apparently fits with the playbook of his
> counsel – of prying into and exploiting Cline's sexual history to
> threaten her, even going so far as to make the false and absurd
> claim that she was an "escort." Reetz-Laiolo and his counsel's ex-
> treme and aggressive campaign against Ms. Cline moved into farce
> when they implied that Reetz-Laiolo's damages from his "injuries"
> could approach "billions" of dollars."

As with Giuffre, it was only after Reetz-Laiolo met lawyers from the
Boies Schiller law firm that he apparently hatched a plan to turn a
frivolous and time-barred legal claim into a big-day payout:

> "Because of the Refog program, which had captured and stored re-
> cords of Cline's computer activity while she owned the computer,
> Reetz-Laiolo has been in possession of a trove of personal infor-
> mation about Cline since he purchased her computer in 2013, in-
> cluding her private correspondence, journal entries, intimate web
> browsing history, and photographs… However…even after he dis-
> covered the Refog program, Reetz-Laiolo did not immediately un-
> derstand the extent of what he had in his possession. It was only in
> 2016, after he began to realize the weakness of his copyright claims
> against Cline, that Reetz-Laiolo realized he could exploit this trove
> of Cline's most personal information. Thereafter, in keeping with
> his long history of using extortionate threats to control. Cline,
> Reetz-Laiolo hatched a plan to exploit this information to shore
> up his wilting copyright claims, and extract a financial windfall
> from Cline and Random House through alternative means… [H]e

---

54 The counter complaint is available here https://32fc87n66z83fzh742e992fv-
wpengine.netdna-ssl.com/wp-content/uploads/2017/11/Clinecomplaint.pdf, found in
Vivia Chen, David Boies Is In Trouble Again with Women, *The Careerist*, Dec. 6, 2017,
available at https://thecareerist.typepad.com/thecareerist/2017/12/boies-in-trouble-
again.html (emphasis added)

threatened to reveal her past use of the Refog software not because he believed he had a credible claim, but in order to extort the maximum financial settlement from Cline."

Although the Boies Schiller law firm knew or should have known that Reetz-Laiolo had no credible legal claim, they went ahead with the lawsuit. As Cline's lawyer recounted:

> On March 30, 2017, Reetz-Laiolo's counsel followed up on their February 21, 2017 letter with a draft complaint setting out their supposed claims detail (the "First Draft Complaint"). In the First Draft Complaint, Reetz-Laiolo and his counsel went far beyond what would be necessary to set out claims based on Cline's use of the Refog software and for copyright infringement. The First Draft Complaint made aggressive, transparently threatening use of personal information Reetz-Laiolo had found in the cache of Refog data that he considered most likely to humiliate Cline. [E]mboldened by a perceived legitimate legal "hook," he and his counsel included in the First Draft Complaint screenshots of Cline highlighting and copying erotic literature from the internet into a document…, alleging that these were a further example of Cline's "plagiarism." However, the First Draft Complaint identified no corresponding instance of any language from the cited erotica appearing in any of Cline's work. These allegations were included in the First Draft Complaint purely to humiliate Cline, and bully her and her publisher into settling for an unreasonable sum rather than have this extraordinarily personal information aired in open court."

If that was not bad enough, the Boies Schiller firm doubled down in their revised draft complaint:

> "A revised draft complaint (the "Second Draft Complaint")…falsely accused Cline of being an "escort," and attempted to sexualize and smear her platonic relationship with a benefactor (who it also named). In short, the Second Draft Complaint, with the imprimatur of the Boies Schiller firm, followed an age-old playbook: it in-

voked the specter of sexual shame to threaten a woman into silence and acquiescence."

This episode was reported on in *The New Yorker*[55] and *The New York Times*[56], and Boies Schiller was criticized for its behavior. (David Boies has just been criticized for his role in the Weinstein case.) Legal ethics scholar Professor Stephen Gillers told *The New Yorker*, "Lawyers can refuse to engage in tactics they find morally repulsive. This is especially true here because the screenshots, even if not entirely extraneous to the dispute, are of barely marginal relevance."[57]

Boies Schiller's General Counsel stated that David Boies had no involvement in the matter: "Boies had nothing to do with the draft or filed complaint, but he did participate in one settlement discussion."[58] However, while Boies' name was omitted from the complaint that was filed, the fact that he used his name in the draft complaint was obviously aimed at intimidating Cline and her lawyers. They refused to settle the case. A California judge ruled in Cline's favor and dismissed Reetz-Laiolo's lawsuit.[59]

If these tactics sound similar to the ones allegedly used by Boies against Wexner, it is because they derive from the Boies "play-book."

Epstein's death will not end the investigations. Among the mysteries that should be explored are whether Giuffre committed perjury when she accused Wexner and other prominent men of having sex with her, or whether Boies engaged in a "shakedown" and/or received hush money for Giuffre to cover up Wexner's alleged crimes.

55 Sheelah Kolhatkar, How the Lawyer David Boies Turned A Young Novelist's Sexual Past Against Her, *The New Yorker*, Dec. 1, 2017.

56 Alexandra Alter, Sex, Plagiarism and Spyware: This Is Not Your Average Copyright Complaint, *New York Times*, Dec. 1, 2017.

57 Sheelah Kolhatkar, How the Lawyer David Boies Turned A Young Novelist's Sexual Past Against Her, *The New Yorker*, Dec. 1, 2017.

58 Vivia Chen, David Boies Is In Trouble Again with Women, *The Careerist*, Dec. 6, 2017, available at https://thecareerist.typepad.com/thecareerist/2017/12/boies-in-trouble-again.html

59 Emma Cline's ex-boyfriend's copyright claim dismissed, *The Guardian*, July 3, 2018. https://www.theguardian.com/books/2018/jul/03/emma-cline-ex-boyfriend-copyright-claim-dismissed-the-girls

CHAPTER 10

The Weaponization of the Media to Defame and Sue

U nsavory lawyers have developed an insidious tactic by which they can falsely accuse innocent people and then sue them for defamation if they deny the false accusations. These lawyers have weaponized the media in aid of this tactic. Some journalists—such as Julie Brown of the *Miami Herald* and Connie Bruck of *The New Yorker*—have worked hand in hand with these lawyers to promote their own careers and ideological interests over a commitment to the truth. This is how this dangerous partnership works: the lawyers pressure a client into making a false accusation, but they are careful to make it *only* in court documents that are protected by the so-called litigation privilege, even if it is irrelevant to the court proceeding, as the Judge ruled it was in my case; this privilege protects anything said in a court document or proceeding from a defamation suit. The false accuser or her lawyers then leaks the judicially protected false accusation to media, which is also protected against a defamation suit for reporting on what was said in court papers or proceedings. The media then publishes the false accusation without requiring the false accuser to repeat the accusation to the journalist outside the protection of the privilege. The false accuser and her lawyers can in this way "launder" defamatory accusations through the media and achieve the same result they would have achieved had they made the accusation directly to the news media, but—and here is the critical element—without incurring the risk of a defamation suit for making a false accusation. Moreover, because the accusation is made in court papers, some readers believe it has the imprimatur of the courts and is, therefore, more credible than if it had been made directly to the media.

The victim of the false accusation then has only three options. The first and most obvious is that he can immediately respond to the media report of the false accusation *in the* media. But his response may not be protected by the litigation privilege, because it is not made in court papers or proceedings. He can, therefore, be sued for defamation for merely denying the accusation and saying it is a lie.

The second option is to respond in court documents or proceedings and thus be protected by the privilege. But filing court papers or appearing in court takes time, and it is imperative to respond to false accusations immediately—within the news cycle—if the denial is to be reported and credited. A court filing made days or weeks after the initial accusation was reported in the media will either not be reported or, if reported, will be buried.

The third option is to ignore or "no comment" the accusation and hope it goes away. An entirely innocent, falsely accused victim should not be satisfied with the story going away. He should categorically deny and disprove the false accusation.

I chose the first option—immediately responding in the media. I went on television and categorically denied the charges and accused my false accuser and her lawyers of making up the entire story. I wrote an op-ed for the *Wall Street Journal* in which I exposed the tactic of the lawyers and warned that what they did to me could be done to other innocent victims, unless something is done to end this abusive tactic. Here is some of what I wrote on January 14, 2015:

> You challenge the . . . lawyers who filed the court document to repeat the false charges in the media, so you can sue them. They remain silent. You challenge the woman, now 31-years-old, to bring rape charges against you and you offer to waive any statute of limitations, because the filing of a false rape charge is itself a serious crime—though it is rarely prosecuted. She doesn't accept your challenge.

And then, sure enough, the lawyers who made the false accusations . . . sue you for defaming them—though they claim you can't sue them for falsely accusing you of a crime.

Welcome to the Kafkaesque world of American justice. But Kafka was writing fiction when he described the ordeal faced by Josef K in his famous novel, "The Trial." What I have described is real. It is happening to me right now. And if it can happen to me, it can happen to anyone.

I then described how I felt:

I may never have the opportunity to prove my innocence, or to have my accusers prove the false charges, in any court of law. But because I am relatively well known—a double-edged sword in these situations—I can at least fight back in the court of public opinion, though at the very high cost—in legal fees, loss of insurance coverage and the possibility of a large monetary judgment against me.

Imagine the same thing happening to a person who did not have the resources to fight back.

Finally, I proposed a remedy:

The law must be changed to shatter this hall of mirrors I face and others might. There must be consequences for those who file accusations with no offer to prove them and no legal responsibility if they are categorically—and disprovably—false.[60]

But the law has not yet been changed, and so the insidious and unfair tactic is still being deployed, with the assistance of the media. It encourages and incentivizes the leveling of knowingly false accusations in court filings that are then deliberately leaked to the media and published by them without any corroboration or on-the-record confirmation. The United States Court of Appeals for the Second Circuit

---

60 Alan M. Dershowitz, A Nightmare of False Accusation That Could Happen to You, *Wall Street Journal*, Jan. 14, 2015.

has, however, recently cautioned the media against allowing itself to be weaponized in aid of this tactic.

Here is the "note of caution," issued by Judge Jose A. Cabranes, "To the public regarding the reliability of court filings." It should be read and acted on by every media publisher, editor, journalist and reader.

> Materials submitted by parties to a court should be understood for what they are. They do not reflect the court's own findings. Rather, they are prepared by parties seeking to advance their own interests in an adversarial process. Although affidavits and depositions are offered "under penalty of perjury," it is in fact exceedingly rare for anyone to be prosecuted for perjury in a civil proceeding.
>
>   . . . .
>
> Moreover, court filings are, in some respects, particularly susceptible to fraud. For while the threat of defamation actions may deter malicious falsehoods in standard publications, this threat is non-existent with respect to certain court filings. This is so because, under New York law [and the law of most other states], "absolute immunity from liability for defamation exists for oral or written statements made . . . in connection with a proceeding before a court." Thus, although the act of filing a document with a court might be thought to lend that document additional credibility, in fact, allegations appearing in such documents *might be less credible* than those published elsewhere.
>
> [T]he media does the public a profound disservice when it reports on parties' allegations uncritically. . . . Even ordinarily critical readers may take the reference to "court papers" as some sort of marker of reliability. *This would be a mistake.*
>
> We therefore urge the media to exercise restraint in covering potentially defamatory allegations, and we caution the public to read such accounts with discernment.[61] (Emphasis added.)

Judge Cabranes's wise caution raises a broader issue of journalistic

---

61   See Cabranes opinion, Brown v. Maxwell, No. 18-2868 (2d Cir. 2019).

ethics. Should the media report an accusation by an accuser in court-protected documents, when the accuser is not prepared to make that accusation on the record, outside the protection of the litigation privilege? The truth or falsity of accusations made in a court pleading cannot generally be tested or challenged in a judicial proceeding. If the accuser is not even willing to make the accusation on the record with a journalist, it seems unfair for that journalist to repeat the accuser's accusation, especially if uncorroborated.

Why would a reporter who is interested in the truth not press an accuser to repeat and defend her accusation on the record? If the accuser refuses, the reporter should, at the very least, report that refusal. (As we see in the pages to come, many journalists do not even do that, especially with #MeToo accusations.)

This issue needs to be debated both within the media and by outside experts.

By publishing accusations made only within the litigation privilege, without requiring the accuser to go on the record, the media encourages deliberately false accusations made out of extortionate, vengeful or other improper motives. Because there are no legal consequences for the accuser—even if the accusation is proved false—such accusations will increase, especially in the current #MeToo era, when it is a political sin to disbelieve a woman, even if there is evidence that she is lying. A heavy burden of proof is on the accused to prove his innocence, and even if he satisfies that burden—as I did—there will be those who continue to believe the accuser.

The media should require all accusers to repeat accusations they made in court submissions to a journalist, on the record, before spreading a potentially false accusation around the world. But they generally don't.

The worst offender in this regard is Julie Brown of the *Miami Herald*. Brown calls herself an investigative journalist, but in reality she is a one-sided polemicist who gets her information not from independent investigations, but rather from adversarial lawyers who are interested in promoting an agenda rather than in reporting complex and nuanced truths.

Her "reporting" on the Epstein case was hand-fed to her by

Virginia Roberts Giuffre's lawyers. They provided her this one-sided information, apparently, in exchange for an understanding that
Brown would "report" only Giuffre's side of the story, which turns out
to be highly questionable in general, and completely made up with
regard to her accusation against me.

Brown interviewed Giuffre for a *Miami Herald* video, but refused
to ask her on camera to repeat her accusation against me. She knew
that Giuffre would not do so. Instead, Brown allowed her to say
she had sex with *unnamed* politicians, businessmen and *academics*.
When Giuffre said the word academics—without specifying me—
Brown flashed *my* photograph on the video screen. She did not report
that Giuffre had refused to go on the record and name me, or that
Brown had a deal with Giuffre's lawyers not to ask her specifically to
name me. Rarely have I seen more irresponsible and unprofessional
"journalism."

I provided Brown with documented evidence of Giuffre's long
history of lying—about the Gores, Clinton, her age and other issues.
I also provided her with detailed evidence of Ransome's lies about
Hillary Clinton and others. Not only did Brown refuse to include
these histories in her reporting, she lied about what I provided her.
Here is what she wrote: "Dershowitz has attacked both women's
credibility, in particular pointing to falsehoods in some of Ransome's
past statements. He says he has proof that both are lying *but has never
presented it publicly.*"[62] This is categorically false. In Appendix N, I
provide one of several emails I sent Brown documenting their history
of lying, as well as documented facts that she refused to include in her
biased reporting.

Among the information I provided her, which she did not publish,
was the following: "overwhelming evidence of Robert's [Giuffre's]
long history or perjury and lying, including her false claims of meeting Al and Tipper Gore and Bill Clinton on Epstein's island," "her
own lawyer's statement that she did not tell the truth about having
sex on multiple occasions with Leslie Wexner," "Roberts deliberately

---

62   Julie Brown, "When you are in, you can't get out." Women Describe How Jeffrey
Epstein Controlled Them, *Miami Herald*, September 20, 2019.

lied about her age to falsely claim that she was underage," Giuffre's claim to have had "sex with George Mitchell, Bill Richardson, Ehud Barak," Rebecca Boylan's statement that Giuffre was "pressured" into naming me, Boies's admission that Giuffre was "simply wrong," and the emails and book manuscript that proved Giuffre had never even met me. When I pressed Brown about these omissions, she responded, "This was not the story."

I invited Brown to review my travel records for as long as she wished. She spent several hours poring over them and then said she had to leave because her "parking meter had run out." I urged her to return to complete her review, but she insisted that she must take my records with her. I believe that the only reason she wanted to take the records with her was to give them to Giuffre's lawyers, so that they could try to find dates when we were both in New York. I repeated my offer to review the records for as much time as she needed and to take as many notes as she wanted. She declined my offer and then falsely reported that I refused to allow her to inspect the records.

Brown also asked me to break the law. Here is our exchange regarding the sealed emails that Sarah Ransome had sent to the *New York Post* claiming she had sex tapes of Hillary Clinton, Donald Trump, Bill Clinton and Richard Branson:

> **Dershowitz:** I'm not permitted to send them. I am subject to a sealing order. She [Ransome] is not subject to that order and she can show them to you. If she refuses, it's because she is hiding something. I would love to send them to you. Ask her and her lawyers whether they consent to have me send them. If they refuse, you should report that.
> **Brown:** Alan, *you can send them.* There are many documents floating around in this case, so I'm sure *no one will go after you.*
> (Emphasis added)

I believe that her reference to "many documents floating around" is an admission that Giuffre's lawyers had already shared sealed documents with her, as I know they have with other journalists with whom they have collaborated. My lawyers cautioned me that the reason she told me I "can send" the sealed documents to her was not because she was interested in reporting their content, which would undercut her narrative, but because she wanted to tell Giuffre's lawyers that I had broken the law by sending her the sealed material. I did not fall for this ploy. I responded to her request to break the law by emailing: "I will comply with the law even if you are asking me to break it."

Brown's one-sided "reporting" earned her great praise, especially from those who were unaware of what she deliberately omitted from her reports.[63] She was proposed for many journalistic awards, including a Pulitzer Prize. I felt an obligation to inform the Pulitzer Committee of her failings as an objective reporter. I wrote an open letter documenting the information I had provided Brown and then wrote the following:

> So how did Pulitzer candidate Brown deal with all this evidence discrediting her primary source? She simply omitted any mention of it and presented Giuffre as an entirely credible witness with no doubts about her truthfulness.
>
> . . .
>
> Brown deliberately mendaciously misled her readers—and the Pulitzer Committee—by choosing to omit from her narrative every single document, sworn testimony and other proof that would raise questions about the credibility of her primary source. She admitted to me in a consensually recorded conversation that there is absolutely no evidence corroborating or supporting Giuffre's accusation against me, but she did not publish that important fact. Nor did she publish the fact that Giuffre refused to accuse me on the record.
>
> This is not journalism. It is advocacy, and it is advocacy that would get a lawyer disciplined for willfully withholding exculpatory evidence. It is also advocacy that hurts the #MeToo movement by encouraging false reports that damage the credibility of an important movement.

---

63 See, e.g., Tiffany Hsu, The Jeffrey Epstein Case Was Cold, Until a *Miami Herald* Reporter Got Accusers to Talk, *New York Times*, July 9, 2019.

Brown did not win the 2019 Pulitzer Prize. Before she is considered for any future prizes, her unprofessional tactics should be thoroughly and fairly investigated—which is more than she has done with regard to Giuffre.

Brown is all too typical of reporting about #MeToo accusations. For her everything is black and white: women accusers *never* lie about *anything*. Men who deny accusations *do lie*. There is no nuance or attempt at balance in her reporting. If there is evidence that a victim is lying, she will simply not report that evidence, regardless of how strong, because it will undercut her simple-minded and one-sided narrative.

Other journalists as well don't dare to report facts that undercut the narrative that women tell the truth and men lie. If they do, or if they decline to publish false accusations by alleged victims, they are criticized by other media. National Public Radio, for example, recently did a segment on ABC TV's decision several years earlier not to run an interview they had conducted with Giuffre. The reporter, David Folkenflik, wrote me the following email:

> I cover media for NPR and wanted to ask—I've been told that you felt you were successful in persuading ABC NEWS's legal team in not running an interview with Virginia Roberts Giuffre in 2015 because you convinced them she was untruthful.

I assumed, therefore, that he was interested in the evidence I provided ABC that "convinced them she was untruthful." But as we shall see, that was the last thing he was interested in reporting. This is what I told Folkenflik about my interaction with ABC.

In mid-2015, I was sent an email that one of Giuffre's lawyers had circulated, announcing that an interview with Giuffre would be run on *Good Morning America*, the ABC evening news and *Nightline*. I immediately called ABC to inquire whether my name was being mentioned. They said it was not. (To this day, she has not publicly and directly accused me out of court, in order to avoid being held accountable for her defamation.) I asked about Leslie Wexner and was told that his name was also not mentioned. (Perhaps because her silence

about him was being negotiated.) I told the producer that Giuffre
had a long history of lying about prominent individuals, including
the Gores and Clinton, as well as about other matters. I also told
them about my conversation with Giuffre's friend Rebecca Boylan,
in which she told me about the plan to obtain a billion dollars from
Wexner. I told them that these interviews with Giuffre were part of
the shakedown plan—that Boylan had told me that Giuffre went on
TV in order to send Wexner the following message: See, I have access to the media; this time I didn't mention you; but next time . . .

The people at ABC said they would look into the matter and I
sent them the evidence. I made it clear that I was calling *only* on
my own behalf and *not* on behalf of Epstein. I told the same thing to
Folkenflik when he interviewed me about this episode. But Folkenflik
had an agenda and a story line, and reporting accurately what I told
him would undercut his pre-determined narrative. So this is what he
falsely reported in a piece entitled "How media fell short on Epstein."[64]
Folkenflik described me as Epstein's lawyer, without disclosing that
I explicitly told him that I had called ABC *only* on my *own* behalf as
someone who had been falsely accused by Giuffre. Notwithstanding
his expressed interest in how I "convinced" ABC not to run the interview, he never mentioned the evidence I provided to ABC and
to *him* proving that Giuffre had a long record of lying. Instead he
quoted Julie Brown *recently* telling him, "I [Brown] found [Giuffre]
to be very truthful and credible." But Brown had never told that to
ABC, back *when they were making their decision.* She only told it to
Folkenflik when he was doing his report years *later.* So her biased and
self-serving after-the-fact assessment of Giuffre's alleged credibility
was completely irrelevant to ABC's decision, while my evidence—
which I sent to ABC *at the time*—was highly relevant. Yet Folkenflik
deliberately omitted my evidence from his reporting.

Accordingly, he made it sound as if ABC had succumbed to pressure from Epstein and his powerful friends rather than making a decision, based on hard evidence they received from me, that Giuffre's

---

64 David Folfenflik, A Dead Cat, A Lawyer's Call and A 5-Figure Donation: How
Media Fell Short on Epstein, NPR, August 22, 2019.

lack of credibility did not satisfy ABC's journalistic standards. This is yet another example of biased and unprofessional journalism—this time by NPR—promoting the credibility of false accusers even in the face of overwhelming evidence that they are lying, and attacking a responsible network for making the right decision based on the evidence they had at the time. This story, too, was fed to NPR by Giuffre's lawyers—an important fact they failed to disclose.

The fear of being criticized for not believing an alleged victim—even one who is a proven liar—resulted in an article being spiked by the *Daily Beast*. I received a call from Lachlan Cartwright of the *Beast*. He had just read the unsealed emails between Giuffre and the journalist Sharon Churcher in which Giuffre essentially admitted that she didn't have sex with me. He expressed outrage at the obvious fact that I was being framed by Giuffre, who had been encouraged by Churcher to include me in her manuscript even though she had never met me. Here is what he messaged me: "Churcher crossed a massive lien [sic, line]. Sharon Churcher inserts your name into Virginia's story . . . and people wonder why [journalism] gets a bad rap." "Churcher stitched you up." "I want to blow this up. I suggest we set the record straight. No one has picked up on these Churcher emails. Have you been contacted by my competitors?" "Churcher and the mos [sic] basically over egged what Virginia Roberts told them, and she was being paid for her story."

I told Cartwright that I blamed Giuffre rather than Churcher and that I had drafted an op-ed making this point. He pleaded with me to let him have the scoop: "No I want to write it," he insisted. "This isn't a column/op-ed. It's a news story." "It's very shoddy journalism . . . its egregious." He told me "It will be much more powerful coming from me and The Beast than coming from you." I agreed to withhold my op-ed pending his article. He asked me to send him relevant material, including the draft of my article and the documentary and recorded evidence, which I did. He told me he would get on it immediately and blow the lid off this frame up, as soon as he received approval from his editor.

That was the last I heard from him. Obviously the editor of the *Daily Beast*—a website that made its reputation by uncritically supporting the narratives of #MeToo victims—did not want to publish a truthful article that undercut the #MeToo narrative by exposing an instance of lying by an alleged victim. To report honestly on Giuffre's false accusation of me was to risk being deemed by some to be disloyal to the movement and to its mantra that women must be believed even in the face of documented evidence that a particular woman made up a false accusation for money. Cartwright has refused to respond to numerous emails and messages. He's obviously ashamed of not publishing an important story he knows is true. The *Beast* should also be ashamed for refusing to report the truth about what they know is a false accusation. To quote Cartwright, "It's very shoddy journalism," and "people wonder why [journalism] gets a bad rap."

Another story fed to the media by Giuffre's lawyers was a "profile" of me in *The New Yorker*[65] that was anything but a profile of my 55-year career and 81-year life. It was a hatchet job calculated to destroy my reputation and silence me.

In March of 2019, my publisher received an email from Connie Bruck, a journalist who writes for *The New Yorker*. She told my publisher that she was "trying to contact" me about a profile, "much of it drawn from [my] books." My publisher gave me her number to call if I wanted to respond. The nature of her email made it clear to me that this was a "cover your ass communication." She said she was "trying" to reach me. She could easily have emailed me directly, since my email is on my website, as is my office phone number. Nearly every criminal in the world has managed to reach me, but Connie Bruck had to go through my publisher. When I called, it became obvious that she had no interest in speaking to me. She said she had completed the profile and would I mind speaking to her fact checkers. I said I never heard of a profile being completed without a face-to-face interview with the subject. She told me she had done several profiles without interviewing the subject. I challenged her: "Isn't it true that in all of those profiles the subjects refused to speak with you?"

---

65   Connie Bruck, Alan Dershowitz: Devil's Advocate, *The New Yorker*, August 5th & 12th

Sheepishly, she acknowledged that that was the case. Well, I wanted to be interviewed in person.

I offered to fly to California to meet with her or have her come East. She refused, but agreed to ask me some questions over the phone. Her questions were all accusatory. It was more like an adversarial deposition than a journalistic interview. It was certainly not a search for truth or balance. She was not interested in my life, my aspirations, my family or my values. She was only interested in confirming her pre-existing negative attitude toward me by asking "gotcha" questions.

I later learned (and wrote) that the negative profile was proposed by Virginia Roberts Giuffre's lawyers in order to promote their case, and that it was approved by *The New Yorker* editor, David Remnick, as a way of silencing me. Both Remnick and Bruck have relationships with Boies, and both despise President Trump, Prime Minister Netanyahu and Israel. Destroying me suited all their agendas, so the project was launched.

Bruck was so determined to dig up dirt on me that one of the first sources she Googled to was Rense.com, a neo-Nazi, Holocaust-denial website which both the Anti-Defamation League and Southern Poverty Law Center have declared to be anti-Semitic. Several years earlier, this site accused me of beating and murdering my first wife. (She died 10 years after we separated and divorced.) It showed "pictures" of her and my children, which were not them, but stereotypical Jews with long noses.

No one would believe anything on this hate site—no one, that is, except a journalist prepared to use any dirt, regardless of its source and absurdity, against her target. Bruck has admitted using this discredited site as the original source for claiming in her article draft that I abused my first wife and "stripped" her of custody of my two sons. She even used the same words she found on the Holocaust Denial site. The truth is that my first wife and I, who were married when I was 20 and she 19, grew apart. There was no abuse, and the court granted me custody based on the report of the social worker, and on his explicit finding that I committed "no misconduct." But that boring story would not achieve *The New Yorker*'s goal of destroying me.

So they went into the gutter and followed the lead of an anti-Semitic website.

When Bruck's article was published, it contained tell-tale evidence of her reliance on this disreputable source. It reported that my first wife "walked to the middle of the Brooklyn Bridge and leapt to her death." Police and medical records prove that that is entirely untrue. It was an invention of Rense.com. After the article appeared online, Bruck was confronted with the evidence and *The New Yorker* agreed to remove her false claim from the online version, though not from the hard copy. She now has to explain why she relied on Rense, without any other evidence or source, to include this false statement in her reporting. The fact checkers never asked about it, even though they asked about many other aspects of my first marriage. This reportorial bias alone is enough to discredit the article, but there were many more egregious errors in her article.

I wrote a letter to *The New Yorker* correcting its errors, but they refused to publish it. They denied that they relied on Rense.com. But there is no other source for the fictional Brooklyn Bridge account (which had appeared subsequent to its original article claiming I had murdered my first wife.).

Finally, the editor agreed to publish the following general letter:

If anyone doubts the political bias of *The New Yorker*, I urge them to compare Jane Mayer's defense of Al Franken with Connie Bruck's screed against me ("Devil's Advocate," August 5th & 12th). Mayer resolves doubts in favor of Franken and against his accusers, whose motives she challenges. Bruck resolves doubts in favor of my false accusers, whose motives she does not doubt, and against me. The difference is that there is evidence that Franken did the things he was accused of, though there are doubts about whether what he did was sufficiently serious to warrant his resignation from the Senate. In my case, there is not a scintilla of evidence to support the false allegations against me by two women who Bruck concedes are "imperfect witnesses," one of whom admits that she invented false accusations against other prominent people.

Let me be categorical: I never met my two accusers; I have never had sex with an underaged person; the accusations against me are totally false.[66]

In the end, *The New Yorker* screed was largely a dud. Its bias—political, ideological and personal—was so evident to most readers that it lacked credibility. It did not silence me.[67] Nor did Meghan McCain, though she tried hard to keep me off TV, because I'm "being accused" of Epstein-related improprieties.

I had earlier been on *The View*, which featured McCain, and had described the evidence of my total innocence. But for McCain, *evidence* of innocence is apparently not enough to overcome *accusations* of guilt.

I wrote an op-ed in response to McCain's McCarthyite guilt by association in which I warned:

Imagine what America would be like if McCain's rule became the norm. Every accused person would be presumed guilty and shut down. Our traditional presumption of innocence would be reversed and a presumption of guilt would be substituted. That is the norm in today's China, Iran, Venezuela and other totalitarian nations that do not operate under the rule of law.

I am sure Meghan McCain would respond by saying that her rule should not apply to all cases, but only to allegations of sexual abuse made by women. But there is no such limiting principle. Once an accusation—even a demonstrably false one—becomes the basis

66 I published the longer letter *The New Yorker* refused to publish on Twitter.

67 After the *New Yorker* article first came out, I published a short reply in the *Jerusalem Post*. Alan Dershowitz, How *The New Yorker* Conducts Journalistic Assassinations, The Jerusalem Post, Aug. 1, 2019. After *The New Yorker* refused to publish my point-by-point rebuttal, I published it myself on Twitter. On Aug 23, 2019, I tweeted "The letter to the editor that *The New Yorker* refused to publish. I offered to shorten it but its editor didn't want its readers to learn the truth about *The New Yorker*'s sloppy and biased journalism and fact checking." Here's the link to my response: https://static1.squarespace.com/static/5b9bc617b10598c88f97b47b/t/5d5fddcbba877b0001fe3852/1566563787545/The+New+Yorker+letter+8+3+2019.pdf

for punitive actions including censorship, there will be no stopping the march toward abolishing the presumption of innocence.

Accepting Meghan McCain's rule would encourage false accusations against political enemies in an effort to censor them. One virulently anti-Israel website acknowledged this weaponization of accusations when it wrote the following: "We have picked up news about the sexual allegations against Dershowitz because Dershowitz is such an outspoken supporter of Israel and the matter has inevitably affected his influence in the foreign policy arena." Others have told me that they are happy that I am being accused because it will silence my voice when it comes to defending the legal rights of President Trump. If an accusation becomes enough to silence a controversial speaker, the inevitable result will be the increased weaponization of false accusations. . . .

As a young man I lived through an age in which accusations were deemed sufficient to keep someone off television and other media. That age was called McCarthyism. Meghan McCain's rule would return us to a terrible time in our history.

So let us maintain the presumption of innocence for all. Let's not let accusations be equated with convictions. Let's assure that every accused person is accorded the due process right to disprove the accusation.

I hope Meghan McCain, who I admire, will reconsider her thoughtless demand that I be banned from television on the basis of an accusation that has been thoroughly disproved and discredited.[68]

McCain apparently refused to reconsider and a tentative invitation for me to appear on *The View* to discuss my book *Defending Israel* was withdrawn.

Even the *Columbia Journalism Review*—the self-proclaimed "voice of journalism"—was willing to violate core journalistic ethics in the service of the #MeToo movement. A reporter named Lyz Lenz called to interview me. She agreed our conversation was off the record.

---

68   Alan Dershowitz, Meghan McCain's Dangerous Demand to Censor Me, *Newsmax*, July 12, 2019.

When I described myself as a "victim" of false accusations by Giuffre and her lawyers, she replied: "You're a rich, white man—you can't be a victim." I responded that she wasn't being an objective reporter. She then screamed at me and said that she was going to put that *on the record* despite her prior agreement that it was off the record: "You don't get to insult me off the record."

She then published my off-the-record criticism of her—a clear violation of the ethical rules of journalism. She then went further and published the false claim that this book—which she had *not* read—will blame "the #MeToo movement for [my] trials."

Of course that is not the case. I am blaming those who abuse the #MeToo movement for the false accusations against me being credited by biased journalists like Lenz.

Lenz then defamed me by falsely accusing me of "rhetorically advocating sex with minors," despite my unambiguous statement that I was making a "constitutional (not moral) argument," that the age of consent should be the same for sex as it is for abortion—an argument several prominent feminists have made.

Some in the media have played a commendable role in starting the #MeToo movement by exposing predatory practices by many men. But the media, in general, has refused to engage in nuanced reporting about those few women and their lawyers who have tried to take advantage of a positive movement to turn it into a self-serving racket of leveling false accusations for profit and revenge. The time has come for the responsible media to investigate plausible claims by victims of false accusations. It will take courage to do so. The *Wall Street Journal* showed the way years ago when it exposed fraudulent accusations of child abuse that had resulted in the imprisonment of innocent owners of day care centers in Massachusetts, California, Washington and other states.[69] This exposé did not hinder the prosecution of real abusers. But it forced prosecutors, parents and journalists to distinguish genuine cases of abuse from fraudulent accusations.

---

69 Dorothy Rabinowitz, Darkness in Massachusetts, *Wall Street Journal*, Jan. 30, 1995. The *Wall Street Journal* also published two op-eds by me relating to the Giuffre accusations.

It was a win-win. It will also be a win-win if the current media were to substitute investigation of actual innocence for presumption of guilt based on accusation alone. Thus far, the media, in general, has refused to play this important investigation and reportorial role.

Chapter 11

I Demand to Be Investigated

When it became clear that I would never be vindicated by the current media because of its insistence on uncritically presenting only the narrative of the alleged victims of sexual abuse, I decided to make a bold move—a move that only a completely innocent person with nothing to hide should ever consider making. I demanded an investigation of me by law enforcement.[70]

This move came in several steps. First, I arranged to meet with prosecutors and investigators in the offices of the United States Attorney for the Southern District of New York and the District Attorney of Manhattan.

I began my meeting with the federal prosecutors and FBI by stating that I am aware that lying, even not under oath, to law enforcement officials is a serious felony punishable by imprisonment.[71] I then said that although I'm not required to deny my guilt, I want to state unequivocally that I never met my accusers and never had any sexual or other contact with them. I could see the FBI agents writing down every word I said. If it were to turn out—as I knew it wouldn't—that I was lying,

---

70 Alan M. Dershowitz, I Want to Be Investigated by the FBI, *Wall Street Journal*, March 21, 2019.

71 18 U.S. Code § 1001.

they would have all the evidence they needed to send me to prison. I then proceeded to lay out the case that Giuffre and her lawyers had tried to frame me as part of an extortion plot against Leslie Wexner. I presented the evidence—including recordings, calendars, testimony and chronology—that demonstrated how Giuffre and her lawyers had falsely accused me *publicly* while at the same time accusing Wexner *secretly* of nearly identical conduct. I told them that both Wexner's wife and lawyer had used the word "shakedown" in describing the efforts by Boies to "resolve" the matter.

The agents took extensive notes of everything I said. The prosecutors came into the room with several volumes of what appeared to be testimony or evidence. Both my lawyer and I surmised that these volumes related to other investigations of Boies the Feds may have been conducting. The media had pointed accusatory fingers at Boies for his role in the Theranos case, involving a fraudulent blood testing start-up on whose board Boies served, while simultaneously acting as the lawyer for the company—a clear conflict of interest. The founder and CEO of the sham company was indicted and there was speculation that she might be flipping on Boies and providing evidence against him.

There was also speculation that Boies might be the subject of an investigation growing out of the misuse of private investigators hired by Boies in the Harvey Weinstein case. The media was also raising ethical and legal questions about Boies's involvement with a corrupt Venezuelan politician and entrepreneur. No one was doubting Boies's *right* to represent these people; it was the *manner* by which he was acting for them that apparently interested investigators.

As usual, the federal prosecutors and agents did not tip their hand. They made it clear that they were there to listen, not to talk. They were cordial, but we left the meeting convinced they believed me, but uncertain about whether they would move forward against Giuffre and her lawyers.

My meetings with prosecutors and agents from the Manhattan District Attorney's office was very different. I presented essentially the same evidence to them as I had to the feds. The chief prosecutor—just below the District Attorney himself, Cyrus Vance—questioned me extensively and asked for more details, which I provided. I played the recordings for them and they agreed that our transcripts of the recorded conversations with Boies and Boylan were accurate.

Then I received a shocking phone call from the Chief prosecutor. He told me that Cyrus Vance had decided to recuse himself and his entire office from the matter because he was too close a friend of David Boies, who had also made significant contributions to his election campaign. They would send the case to a different District attorney's office—perhaps in Queens or Staten Island who would take over the investigation and be in touch with me.

I began to prepare a packet of evidence to bring to whichever District Attorney's office took over the case, when I received another, even more shocking call, from the Manhattan prosecutor. Cyrus Vance had changed his mind! He was un-recusing himself and his office and would decide whether to prosecute Boies and Giuffre for extortion and related crimes.

Not surprisingly, Vance decided not to further investigate or prosecute Boies. The reason they gave was that Wexner refused to cooperate. I responded that victims of extortion rarely if ever want to cooperate, especially if the sins or crimes they paid hush money to hush up had not been exposed. This was the situation with Wexner. Following his meeting with Boies, Wexner's name disappeared from the case. Why would he want the accusations against him to be made public, as they would inevitably be, if Boies and Giuffre were to be put on trial for extortion, attempted extortion, or conspiracy to extort?

Finally, after not hearing anything from the Feds and being told that there would be no action by the Manhattan District Attorney's office, I decided to go public. I published a provocative op-ed in the *Wall Street Journal* entitled: "I Want to Be Investigated by the FBI."[72]

My op-ed began as follows:

"If you are accused of a crime, you are entitled to the presumption of innocence. But in the age of #MeToo, people accused of sexual

---

72   Alan M. Dershowitz, I Want to Be Investigated by the FBI, *Wall Street Journal,* March 21, 2019.

misconduct are subjected, at least in the court of public opinion, to
a presumption of guilt. Worse, a claim of innocence-even a prov-
able one-is itself treated as an offense, an assault on the accuser and
on "survivors" in general."

I then observed:

"Yet there are some in the #MeToo movement for whom there is
no such thing as innocence. Despite having proved I never even
met my accuser, my appearances on college campuses have been
greeted with protests accusing me of being part of a "rape culture."
People on Twitter have called me a child rapist and worse. There
were calls on social media for Harvard to strip me of the emeritus
status I earned after 50 years of teaching without a single complaint".

I concluded the op-ed with my challenge:

"I've decided, therefore, to do something unusual: I'm asking federal prosecutors and the Federal Bureau of Investigation to open a
criminal investigation of me. But not of me alone—of my accusers
as well. [They] have filed sworn affidavits in federal court. These
affidavits are in irreconcilable conflict: I have sworn that I never
met either of them; they have both sworn that I engaged in sexual
acts with them. Either I have committed perjury or they have.

Someone has committed a serious felony, a crime against
America's justice system. I'm asking law-enforcement authorities to
figure out who. I will cooperate, showing them my evidence, testify-
ing before the grand jury, invoking no privileges. I will challenge my
accusers to do the same. It's no fun to be investigated for a felony by
the FBI, but the current state of the law and public opinion gives me
no alternative if I want to be vindicated.

In more than half a century of litigating criminal cases, I have
never seen one in which the evidence of innocence is so incontrovertible and the evidence of guilt nonexistent. If my evidence is

"inconclusive," then no falsely accused person can ever clear his name."

The sad reality is that some of my critics believe I am guilty despite this evidence. They conflate my representation of Epstein—and helping to get him what some regard as a sweetheart plea bargain—with the false accusation that I had sex with Epstein's victims. But the two are completely different. I did what the law and legal ethics oblige me to do in my role as Epstein's lawyer. I did what I'm accused of: namely, helping him get the best possible deal. All lawyers should seek that once they decide to represent a client. And in my opinion no good lawyer should refuse to represent a client because he is despised and accused of heinous crimes. In representing a client, the lawyer must, of course, play by the rules, both ethical and legal, which I have done.

In contrast, I have never engaged in illegal sexual behavior, or improperly touched any female associated with Epstein (or anyone else). Of those false charges I am totally innocent and a victim of perjuriously false accusation.

So the two accusations—that I represented Epstein, and that I had sex with anyone associated with him—should never be conflated or confused. The first was the right thing to do and I did it. The second would have been the wrong thing if I had done it. But I didn't do it.

For some thoughtless critics, the fact that I represented Epstein makes it more likely that I had sex with his victims. To the contrary, if I had engaged in improper sex with anyone associated with Epstein in 2001 or 2002—which I did not—I never would have agreed to represent him in 2005 and 2006 and be in the limelight as his lawyer. The fact that I successfully represented him does, however, make it far more likely that I would be subjected to a false accusation by one his victims, angry at me for helping Epstein get a "sweetheart" deal which denied her "justice." Both of my false accusers have acknowledged that they despise me and wish me ill for having represented Epstein, thus providing a motive—in addition to the financial motive—for falsely accusing me. I, on the other hand, have no motive to attack them other than to clear my name of false accusations. I do not know them, have never met them and have nothing against them other than that they have falsely accused me, which is quite a lot.

We live in such a polarized world today that there are even some who conflate my controversial support for President Trump's constitutional rights with the accusations against me of sexual misconduct. As one person put it to me: "Anyone who does anything that helps Trump has no morals, so I can believe you'd do anything." Another said: "I was hoping you were guilty of the sex stuff, because that would have shut you up about Trump, but damn it, the evidence proves you didn't do it, so I guess you'll keep blabbering about Trump." An anti-Israel website expressly associated accusations of sexual misconduct with my defense of Israel: "We have picked up news about the sexual allegations against Dershowitz because Dershowitz is such an out-spoken support of Israel and the matter has inevitably affected his influence in the foreign policy area."[73]

* * *

I welcome a full and fair investigation. It may be the only way—in this #MeToo age of presumed guilt—to finally and fully prove that I am the totally innocent victim of false and perjurious accusations.

---

73   Philip Weiss, Dershowitz's Comments Are 'Shockingly Vicious and Sexist' Says *Harvard Law Record* Article, MondoWeiss, Feb. 19, 2015.

CHAPTER 12

Being Sued for Telling the Truth:
A Grave Danger to the First Amendment

In March of 2019, Virginia Roberts Giuffre sued me for defaming her by denying her false accusations and calling her a liar and perjurer. Julie Brown, the so-called journalist, who was working hand in hand with David Boies and Giuffre's other lawyers, knew about the law suit before I did. She was shown the complaint before it was filed and had a lengthy story ready to go. She also helped Giuffre's lawyers gather information from me on the pretext that she was acting as a journalist, anxious to see my evidence, rather than as an investigator helping Giuffre's lawyer in suing me.

The lawsuit itself violated the spirit if not the letter of the First Amendment by asking the court to punish me for denying a false accusation. If every public figure were sued for denying accusations—false or true—and calling his accuser a liar, the courts would be so filled with defamation suits that they would have little time for anything else. Think about all the times current politicians, from the president on down, have called their political opponents liars or have accused them of making up stories about them. I remember when Adlai Stevenson promised that if his opponent stopped lying about him, he would stop telling the truth about his opponent.

From the beginning of our history as a nation, the word liar has been bandied about by politicians, journalists, academicians and ordinary folks. Jefferson, Hamilton, Burr, Jackson, Lincoln, Roosevelt, Kennedy, Johnson, Carter, Reagan, Clinton, Obama and Trump have been called liars and some have responded in kind. J. Edgar Hoover called Martin Luther King the "most notorious liar in the country."

A simple check of Google will show that others who have been called "liars" include the following: Ralph Nader, Nancy Pelosi, Al Sharpton, George W. Bush, Jesse Jackson, Eric Holder, Adam Schiff, John Kerry, Ted Cruz, Al Gore, Elizabeth Warren, Loretta Lynch, Henry Kissinger, Barney Frank, Michelle Obama, Condoleezza Rice, Antonin Scalia, Brett Kavanaugh, Clarence Thomas, Phil Murray, John Lewis, and Michael Bloomberg. There are even websites that catalogue those who have been called liars.

Rarely has the person called a liar responded by suing. The expected response is in the marketplace of ideas or in the development of a thicker skin, especially by those who initiated the exchange of verbal epithets by hurling the accusation in the first place. It was Sigmund Freud who declared that the beginning of civilization can be marked by the first person who hurled an insult instead of a spear. In the old days, a person falsely accused of a sex crime might challenge his accuser to a duel. Today, they should be free to call the accuser a liar, as I did. That's how the marketplace of ideas—and epithets— works. The word liar has become so overused that it has lost its sting and its power to inflict damage on the person accused of lying.

Giuffre's lawyers know this, so it is unlikely that the real purpose of the defamation suit was actually to prevail in court or to obtain damages. There couldn't possibly be any damages since I have been calling Virginia Roberts Giuffre a liar and perjurer since the beginning of 2015, when she first falsely accused me. The statute of limitations is one year, and so the damages would only be for what I have said during the past year, not before that. But I said nothing different during the past year than I said for the previous four years.

Moreover, it is clear from Giuffre's own words that I told the truth when I called her a liar, and truth is an absolute defense to defamation. Giuffre will have to admit that she lied when she made up stories about Tipper Gore, Al Gore and Bill Clinton; when she claimed that she was below the age of consent at the time she was allegedly trafficked by Epstein; when she said her manuscript, in which she names the real names with whom she claimed to have had sex, was intended to be fictional. She has told many other lies as well, so truthfully calling her a liar and a perjurer is not defamatory and could not have caused her any material damages.

I will argue that Giuffre became a public figure when she sold her story for $160,000 and peddled her manuscript seeking a big advance. She also deliberately thrust herself into the limelight by accusing me and others of sexual misconduct and having these accusations leaked to the press. Her recent appearances in front of TV cameras on the courthouse steps and her network and newspaper interviews confirm her status as a public figure subject to the more daunting legal criteria for prevailing in a defamation suit. She didn't become a public figure by being a victim. She became a public figure by exploiting her alleged victimization for profit, publicity and revenge. Public figures don't win defamation suits based on being called a liar when they initiated the verbal exchange by falsely calling their accuser a pedophile.

Giuffre's lawyers have argued that I did not have the constitutional right to defend myself against an accusation that I was a "pedophile" by calling my false accuser a "liar." Here are their exact words: "Dershowitz's statements fall outside of any privilege because they are *disproportionate* to any statement he was responding to." (Emphasis added.) I quote their exact words because no reasonable reader would actually believe that any rational lawyer would actually argue that calling a person a "liar" who accused you of being a "pedophile" is a disproportionate response. In any event, Giuffre also called me a "liar," and so me calling her a liar cannot be deemed a "disproportionate" response. The courts are not the appropriate institution to rule on "liar, liar, pants on fire" exchanges.

Giuffre's lawyers have also argued that the mere denial of a sexual assault constitutes defamation. Here is what they said, quoting a prior opinion by a district court judge:

"[T]o suggest an individual is not telling the truth about her history of being sexually assaulted as a minor constitutes more than a general denial, it alleged something deeply disturbing about the character of an individual willing to be publicly dishonest about such a reprehensible crime."[74]

If the courts were to rule that I had no First Amendment right to "suggest" that Giuffre is not telling the truth about me, such a ruling would establish a dangerous constitutional precedent. It would chill the exercise of free speech and incentivize politicians and others to clog the courts with defamation suits rather than responding to accusations of lying in the marketplace of ideas. It would also encourage lawyers to engineer defamation suits by employing the sleazy tactic used against me: namely, defaming me from behind the litigation privilege and then suing me for truthfully denying the false accusations in public.

In my opinion, the real purpose of the law suit was threefold: first, to defame me and lie about me in the pleadings, on the assumption that these pleadings are protected from defamation lawsuits; second, to punish me economically by requiring me to spend money on legal fees and heightened insurance premiums and to take time from the other work I am doing; third, to try to get me to settle, in the way that Epstein settled his cases, giving the plaintiffs and their lawyers a windfall. Before those suits were settled, I had volunteered to testify against Giuffre and Ransome and prove they had lied about me and so their credibility was in question. But I had no control or influence over Epstein's decisions and the cases were settled, presumably not for financial reasons, but out of concern for what might come out at a trial. I have no such concerns, because I have done nothing wrong and have nothing to hide.

Notwithstanding the illegitimate purposes behind filing the defamation suit, if it were to go to trial, I would be able to subpoena material that is currently either sealed or hidden, and my lawyers would be able to cross-examine Giuffre about her numerous lies and about the emails and manuscript that prove that she never met me or had sex with me. I would also be able to introduce my detailed travel and other records that prove I could not have been on Epstein's island,

---

74 Giuffre v. Maxwell, 165 F. Supp. 3d 147, 152 (S.D.N.Y. 2016).

ranch and other places at which she falsely claims to have met me. Finally, if Giuffre claims under oath in front of a federal judge and jury in a federal courthouse that she ever had sex with me, she will be subjecting herself to criminal perjury charges. I will truthfully swear under oath that I never met her. One if us will be committing perjury in a federal courtroom—an intolerable situation if not investigated and prosecuted. Accordingly, I have asked the FBI to attend the trial and to investigate which one of us is the criminal. The evidence will show it is her.

Some of my critics have alleged that I am being inconsistent by raising First Amendment objections to the defamation action, since I invited a law suit in order to prove my innocence. But there is nothing inconsistent about seeking both goals: the right to defend myself under the First Amendment in the court of public opinion against false accusations; *and* the right to prove my innocence in the courts of law, if my First Amendment rights—and those of all Americans—are compromised in the name of the #MeToo movement.

On October 16th, 2019, Judge Loretta Preska ruled that it was for the jury to determine whether my statements denying Giuffre's accusations and calling her a liar and perjurer come within the First Amendment's self-defense privilege. I am confident that a jury, hearing all the evidence, will conclude that I am telling the truth when I say I never met her. We raised the First Amendment issue in a motion to dismiss in order to preserve it for trial and possible appeal. I look forward to a resolution that both protects my First Amendment right to defend myself against false charges, and that totally exculpates me from any suspicion that I ever met this false accuser.

CONCLUSION

It Could Happen to You!

What have I learned from being falsely accused of heinous crimes by women I never even met? After more than half a century of representing hundreds of accused defendants—some of whom were guilty, others innocent—I finally learned what it actually feels like to be a totally innocent and falsely accused defendant. Although I haven't been accused of any crime by a prosecutor and don't face a criminal prosecution, in some ways it's worse to be accused by an individual woman in the age of #MeToo. A criminal defendant has the opportunity prove that he is not guilty. A man falsely accused of sexual misconduct by a woman has far less opportunity.

* * *

I know I did absolutely nothing criminal or even wrong. I'm proud of the way I've conducted my private and professional life during my long career as a professor, lawyer and public intellectual. But many people, mostly strangers, actually believe—despite overwhelming evidence to the contrary—that I had sex with Virginia Roberts Giuffre when she was underage, and with Sarah Ransome when she was 22. The social media are replete with tweets and messages calling me a "pedophile," a "baby-f..ker," and a "pervert." It's a horrible feeling to know that people not only believe—they "know"—that I did something that I myself would regard as reprehensible.

In the introduction to this book, I asked the reader "simply to assume"—*before* seeing the evidence—my innocence, in order to "imagine how you would feel" if falsely accused. Now that the reader has been presented with the indisputable evidence of my innocence and the total absence of any evidence of guilt, that assumption should become a certainty. Every reasonable reader should agree that I am the victim here—the victim of a perjurious frame-up by women with long and continuing histories of lying for money about prominent men. Readers should also agree that these women, Giuffre and Ransome, as well as their lawyers, should be investigated for the roles they played in these criminal activities.

Yet, there will be some who will be unwilling or unable to disbelieve a false accusation by a woman, regardless of the evidence and lack thereof. There will be others—like the reporter from the *Daily Beast*—who know I have been falsely accused but lack the courage to take on the #MeToo movement even in a case as clear as mine. If my evidence is not enough, then no evidence will ever be enough to prove innocence. If this state of evidence is allowed to become the new basis for determining guilt, then we will surely have moved to an age of guilt by accusation, rather than by proof.

The important lesson for all Americans is that if this can happen to me—if I can be falsely accused and have my reputation tarnished by a frame-up plot with no evidentiary support—it could happen to anyone: to you, to your son, to your father, and even to your daughter.

I have the resources and the determination to fight back and to clear my name, though it has cost me a small fortune. David Boies has told people that even if he can't defeat me in court, he can "bankrupt" me with legal fees. He and his giant law firm have the capacity to bankrupt individual opponents by filing frivolous or insubstantial lawsuits. They have a sordid history of bullying, of conflicts of interest and of other ethical violations.[75] Boies will stop at nothing to even perceived scores, even if it hurts his law firm, as his vendetta

---

75   See discussions of Emma Cline case in Chapter 9.

against me has done, much to the chagrin of several of Boies's partners, who are furious at him for what one has characterized as his "Ahab-like obsessions with killing the white whale"—namely me.

They know that I will do everything legal and ethical to clear my name and prove his complicity with evil. If he and his clients are allowed to get away with their plot to falsely accuse me, it would open the door to more false accusations against innocent people who do not have the resources to fight back.

The Federal court has now ruled that Boies and his law firm are disqualified from representing Giuffre against me. Boies will be a crucial witness in my trial. If he tells the truth, he will be a witness to my total innocence, and the falsity of the accusations against me.

This is everyone's battle, not just mine. It is a battle for justice for all. It is a struggle against those who bear false witness. The Bible commands, "Justice, justice shall you pursue." The word justice is repeated, because there must be justice *both* for the victim of false accusations *and* for those who falsely accuse. I will not rest until "justice" comes to me, as well as to those who have borne false witness against me.

Appendices

APPENDIX A: BOIES'S HISTORY OF CONFLICTS OF INTEREST

David Boies' Long History of Conflicts of Interest

David Boies and his firm have a long and sordid history of conflicts of interest and other ethical violations, which should rebut any future suggestion by Boies that any violations of the Rules of Professional Conduct by them were isolated, inadvertent, and never to be repeated.

Misconduct in Representation of Bruce Winston

In 2003, David Boies and fellow New York attorney Edward Wohl represented Bruce Winston, the son of New York jeweler Harry Winston, in a dispute with Bruce's brother over the Florida portion of an inheritance from their parents.

Together, Wohl and Boies participated in the drafting of an agreement under which a former employee of Winston Jewelers would provide assistance in the litigation for $500 per hour. In addition, the former employee would receive a potential "bonus" of between $100,000 and $1,000,000 depending on "the usefulness of the information provided" which would be paid after a "culmination event" related to the dispute's outcome. The former employee later testified at deposition and was listed as a potential witness by the Winston estate's personal representative and by Bruce Winston's attorneys.

The Florida Bar subsequently brought a charge against Wohl alleging that Wohl offered a witness an inducement to testify falsely. The New York Bar brought a parallel charge against Boies alleging violation of a similar but not identical rule applicable to members of the New York State Bar.

The Florida referee rejected Wohl's claim that the former employee was a consultant, concluding that she was a fact witness because her value to Bruce Winston's case was based on "what she had seen, heard, and experienced while working at the family business." The referee also found that the payments were an inducement and that the bonus payment was particularly significant because the amount of payment to her appeared to turn on the usefulness of her testimony.

The Florida Supreme Court suspended Wohl for 90 days. In doing so, it characterized the offering of financial inducements as "extremely serious misconduct" and the tempting of a witness to color testimony as "an evil that should be avoided."[1]

Boies, despite his direct participation with Wohl in the drafting of the agreement with the former Winston Jewelers employee, avoided bar discipline only because he was not a member of the Florida Bar. As a member solely of the New York Bar, and with the only complaint filed against him being in New York, Boies' behavior was subject only to discipline by the New York Bar.

---

[1] David Horrigan, "90-Day Ban for Jewelry Heir's Attorney," *The National Law Journal* (no date)

David Boies' Representation of Amy Habie
In 2003, David Boies was the subject of an ethics complaint based on his financial support of a lawsuit involving a lawn care company owned by a Boies Schiller Firm's financial officer, Amy Habie, "a woman who was rumored to be… Boies's girlfriend."[2]

The trial judge filed a complaint with the Florida Bar alleging Boies of providing financial assistance to clients. The Florida Bar, in turn, filed a formal ethics charge against Boies. The judge sitting as referee in the disciplinary case ultimately determined that the Florida Rules did not prohibit the type of financial support Boies provided to Habie.[3]

Adelphia, Tyco International, and Qwest Communications Conflict of Interest Scandal
In 2005, it was revealed in the course of a bankruptcy proceeding that Boies had failed to disclose a direct conflict of interest to clients when he recommended that they engage the services of three data and document management services owned in part by his children.

One client, Adelphia Cable, objected to being billed $7 million by companies owned by the Boies children without being informed of the children's ownership interests. As a consequence of Boies' unethical non-disclosure, he was required to step down from his position as Adelphia's special counsel.

At least six other Boies clients, including Tyco International and Qwest Communications, were referred by Boies to companies owned by his children without Boies disclosing their ownership interests. Together, Tyco and Qwest paid between $5 million and $10 million to Boies owned companies for storing and managing legal documents.[4]

The Boies Schiller Firm is Sanctioned for Ignoring a "Blatant" Conflict of Interest in New York
In 2012, the Boies Schiller Firm was cited for a "blatant" conflict of interest in *Madison 92nd Street Associates LLC. v. Marriott International, Inc. et. al.*, (S.D.N.Y. Case No. 1:13-cv-00219). In that case, the Boies Schiller Firm represented Madison 92nd Street

---

[2] Karen Donovan, "v. Goliath: The Trials of David Boies," *Pantheon Books*, New York: 2007, p.330. For further information regarding Boies' involvement with Habie, see Marc Morano, "Gore Recount Lawyer Faces Ethics Sanctions", *CNS News*, July 7, 2008; Paul Barrett, "Few Cravath Partners Regret the Departure of David Boies", *The Wall Street Journal*, May 22nd, 1997

[3] For further information regarding the ethical issues raised by Boies and the Boies Schiller Firm representing Habie and her lawn care company, see Jonathan Glater, "How a Well-Known Lawyer's Firm Got a Black Eye in a Little-Known Case in Florida", *The New York Times*, May 5, 2005; James Grimaldi, "For Defense Teams, Bad News Means billable Hours and Good Profits", *The Washington Post*, August 13, 2001

[4] For further information regarding the Boies Schiller Firm's conflict of interests related to its partnership with companies owned by Boies' children see: Robert Frank and Nathan Koppel, "Boies Office Sent Clients to 3rd Firm with Family Ties", *The Wall Street Journal*, October 11, 2005; Nathan Koppel, "Judge Orders Probe Into Boies Firm", *The Wall Street Journal*, February 8, 2006; Laurie P. Cohen and Robert Frank, "More Boies Clients Used Family Firm", *The Wall Street Journal*, August 31, 2005

Associates in its claim against Marriott International and Host Hotels. Madison 92nd's claim revolved around allegations that Marriott and Host Hotels had participated in an illegal conspiracy formed as part of a settlement agreement between the parties ten years earlier.

The Boies Schiller Firm had represented Host Hotels in the dispute with Marriott ten years earlier, and the firm had made a special presentation to Host's board on the terms of that settlement.

The United States District Court for the Southern District of New York identified a conflict of interest in the Boies Schiller Firm's representation of Madison 92nd's claim against Host Hotels. In her opinion, Judge Colleen McMahon wrote: "A clearer conflict of interest cannot be imagined. A first year law student on day one of an ethics course should be able to spot it. BSF, which holds itself out as one of the country's preeminent law firms, did not." Judge McMahon added that it should have taken the Boies Schiller Firm "but a moment" to realize that its position in the Madison suit was untenable.

The court sanctioned the Boies Schiller Firm, ordering it to pay Host over $270,000 in legal expenses it incurred in having the Boies Schiller Firm disqualified from representing Madison.

Theranos Conflict of Interest Scandal
David Boies and the Boies Schiller firm have long-standing ties with Theranos, a blood testing start-up. In early 2016, questions were raised in the media and by federal regulators about Theranos' technology that have caused its value to plummet. In the wake of these allegations, Boies joined Theranos as a director while at the same time acting as its lawyer in fighting these recent allegations about its technology.[5]

According to some accounts, Boies' holding these two positions simultaneously created a conflict of interest: as Theranos's lawyer, Boies represented the company, as its director, he represented the company's shareholders. In November of 2016, Boies and his firm severed all ties with Theranos, reportedly over disagreements about legal strategies regarding its technology.[6]

---

[5] Steven Davidoff Solomon, "Boies Dual Roles at Theranos Set Up Conflict, *New York Times*, February 2nd, 2016
[6] See John Carreyrou, "Theranos and David Boies Cut Legal Ties", *Wall Street Journal*, November 20th, 2016.

APPENDIX B: MEMO AFTER BOIES MEETING

Meeting with David Boies on June 1 between 10 am and 1 pm.

I have just left a meeting with David Boies which ended with a private conversation in which he said "the lawyers who put your name in the federal pleading, not only did a stupid think that hurt their clients, they also did the wrong thing. They never should have accused you of so heinous a crime without checking and double checking, the way I did with the person I called."

At the meeting itself, Sigrid McCauley, David Stone, Nicholas Maisel and another woman from the Boies firm were present. Boies said his goal was to persuade Virginia Roberts that she was mistaken in identifying me as a person with whom she had sex. He said he thinks that she actually believes that, but she is mistaken. I challenged his view that she actually believes she had sex with me, pointing to the fact that she has also said that she had dinner with Bill Clinton and Al Gore and his wife on the island. David responded by saying "I have never challenged Virginia with regard to her statements about Al and Tipper Gore and I am not vouching for her general credibility, but I think she has come to believe the story about you.

Boies reviewed our documents, focusing on several months during two years. He asked Nick numerous questions and requested that he be shown the original records, especially cell phone records. He said that the records were very persuasive, very complete and very compelling. I told him that we could provide even more documentation, and that what he had seen was merely a work in progress. He said that the more complete the records the better he would be able to persuade VR and her other lawyers that it was impossible that I could be the person with whom she had six sexual encounters on the island, New Mexico, the airplane and Epstein's home in Palm Beach and New York. He seemed particularly shocked when I told him that Virginia had sworn that she gave Epstein oral sex while I stood next to him talking to him. He asked Sigrid to show him the affidavit in which she made that claim and he seemed to be shocked by it.

. . .

The meeting was entirely amicable.

Appendix C: Transcripts of Conversations with Rebecca Boylan

Conversations with Rebecca Boylan

Tape A

Alan M. Dershowitz: Now turning on a tape recorder and I'm recording with uh your permission. So please repeat what you told me previously.

Rebecca: Okay, um that Virginia never wanted to go after you um but she felt pressure um by her lawyers and that she had never... I've never heard her mention you as when we were kids or you know until very recently after everything has happened in the media but I've never heard her mention you before.

Alan M. Dershowitz; Okay thank you and I'm turning off the tape recorder. Thank you so much.

Tape B

Alan M. Dershowitz: [inaudible] record and where you repeat what you basically said to me before about the uh man in Columbus and um what he um and how they intended to get the amount of money they intended to get from them. That's crucial. So can you give me that for just like 30 seconds?

Rebecca: Okay, I mean she never told me his name. I know it from you saying it.

Alan M. Dershowitz: We know his name of course.

Rebecca: Okay...

Alan M. Dershowitz: Tell me how she described him to you.

Rebecca: She just said that he owned Victoria Secret and Limited Too, and that he had lots and lots of money. You know, was a billionaire.

Alan M. Dershowitz: Great. And what did they want to do?

Rebecca: They wanted to sue him for at least half his money and use it for the charities that they're trying to start.

Alan M. Dershowitz: And what would the lawsuit be based on?

Rebecca: Oh I guess the... she didn't say exactly, just being affiliated with Epstein the alleged you know and partaking you know in the girls that he would provide them or provide him.

Alan M. Dershowitz: Yeah. And did they think they would have to bring the lawsuit or would they just be able to threaten the lawsuit and he would pay the money?

Rebecca: She made it sound like to me that they were already talking to him and they were, they had already you know in the process of suing him.

Alan M. Dershowitz: Aha. And was he going to then you think settle it or was he actually going to litigate it... what did it sound like?

Rebecca: She didn't really say but she made it sound like she as pretty positive about it and then I didn't hear about it for like months and then you know the last time she talked about the charity, it wasn't about him anymore, it was about just you know raising money going to like you know celebrity charity events to get money or I remember her you know showing she was going to do a bunch of television interview um to raise the... and use that money that they were paying her for the interviews to help get it started.

Alan M. Dershowitz: Right but that would be...

Rebecca: And the lawyers contributed their own money into it probably like, I don't know, like $80,000 or something like that.

Alan M. Dershowitz: They contributed $80,000 to what, to the fund?

Rebecca: The charity yeah, to get it started for her.

Alan M. Dershowitz: And were the lawyers charging her or how did that work... do you know?

Rebecca: Nope, I mean, uh, she, to her, I think the result of her, or what do you call it, pro bono, they weren't charging anything for their, ya know.

Alan M. Dershowitz: But did they expect to get something out of it if they sued this rich guy in Columbus from Victoria Secret.

Rebecca: Really, it's, she didn't say it exactly but that's just kind of like, you know, looking at it in retrospect, that's how it seemed, you know, it just seemed like it was, they saw an opportunity to make a lot of money.

Alan M. Dershowitz: And did she mention, she didn't mention who the lawyers are or where they were from did she?

Rebecca: No. I just have that paperwork that was sent to me by... from them.

Alan M. Dershowitz: right. Sure. But do you know who sent it to you?

Rebecca: Um, she sent, I mean, no, I don't know exactly, she sent it to me... it was forwarded from her email to my email.

Alan M. Dershowitz: Right. And my understanding is that she was going to try to get the uh ABC to uh give her some credibility so that that would increase the leverage on being able to get a settlement or a lawsuit?

Rebecca: Yeah, I mean...

Alan M. Dershowitz: Yeah, alright, well I appreciate that and again just repeat you gave me permission to record this and um would you just say yes so?

Rebecca: Okay, yes.

Alan M. Dershowitz: I appreciate that. Thank you. If you can think of anything else, just please, please let me know because um this is very, very important.

Tape C

Alan M. Dershowitz: I'm recording now with your permission so just tell me the story as as simply as you can.

Rebecca: Okay about the interaction that I had with her where she told me about what was going to happen when it came to starting this charity?

Alan M. Dershowitz: Right.

Rebecca: ... is what you're asking?

Alan M. Dershowitz: Yeah, yeah.

Rebecca: Okay. Um you want me to talk now.

Alan M. Dershowitz: Yeah, sure.

Rebecca: Ok alright, earlier we were together on Clemantis we had dinner at Dempsey's and she just kind of told me about how she was going to sue the man who owned Limited Too and Victoria Secret for lots of money and that they were going to be able to take that money and start this charity to help you know women that had been trafficked and that you know there were other big names that she was going to be able to um also um refer to what happened or what she said had happened when she was younger. Uh I don't know exactly what else. She didn't really mention names just one, just the one that I don't remember his, the guy who owns, you know, Victoria Secret and all that and uh she also said to me that when it came to Alan Dershowitz that she did feel pressure to go after you, after him... um her, you know to, she felt pressure to do it, she didn't want to go after you specifically, that she felt pressured by her lawyers to do that.

Alan M. Dershowitz: Alright, well thank you very much I really appreciate it. You know, we were recording this with your permission. I'm going to turn off the recording now.

APPENDIX D: FIGUEROA AFFIDAVIT

IN THE CIRCUIT COURT OF THE
SEVENTEENTH JUDICIAL CIRCUIT
IN AND FOR BROWARD COUNTY, FLORIDA

CASE NO.: CACE 15-000072

EDWARDS, *et al.*,

    Plaintiffs / Counterclaim Defendants,

    v.

DERSHOWITZ,

    Defendant / Counterclaim Plaintiff.

_____/

AFFIDAVIT OF ANTHONY FIGUEROA

1. My name is Anthony Figueroa. I make this declaration on personal knowledge, voluntarily and without compensation.

2. I first met Virginia Roberts at Royal Palm Beach High School in Royal Palm Beach, Florida where we both attended school. Virginia and I were friends during high school, as were Virginia and my sister.

3. Virginia and I were in a romantic relationship and lived together from sometime in 2000, I cannot recall the specific month, until September 2002. I lived with Virginia Roberts in an apartment that was in her name, although it was my understanding that it was paid for by her then-boss, Jeffrey Epstein. Our relationship ended when Virginia decided not to come back from her trip to Thailand in September 2002.

4. During our approximate two-year romantic relationship, Virginia was Jeffrey Epstein's personal masseuse and would stay or travel with him approximately two weeks out of every month. From the beginning of our relationship I assumed that Virginia's role as a masseuse for Jeffrey Epstein involved sexual acts with Jeffrey Epstein. Virginia did not hide what was going on and was also bringing in a lot of money, which was one of the reasons her involvement with Jeffrey Epstein did not bother me. Towards the end of our relationship, I understood that she was providing massages less frequently or not at all, and instead Jeffrey Epstein had her focused more on recruiting other girls to provide massages.

5. At various times while we lived together, Virginia would tell me the names of famous people whom she said were friends with Jeffrey Epstein. She would also tell me the names of famous people that she saw in Jeffrey Epstein's homes or planes.

6. Virginia only once mentioned Alan Dershowitz as she was listing famous people who were friends of Jeffrey Epstein. I remember during this same conversation she listed certain famous people like President Clinton, Kevin Spacey, and Chris Tucker. Virginia described Mr. Dershowitz as "OJ Simpson's lawyer." She did not say she had ever had any physical contact with him. As I have said before, she had never mentioned anything about them having sex, or brought up anything like that. The first time I heard about Virginia's sexual allegations against Mr. Dershowitz was after the court filling in January 2015 when the media started contacting me for interviews.

I understand that I am swearing or affirming under oath to the truthfulness of the claims made in this affidavit and that the punishment for knowingly making a false statement includes fines and/or imprisonment.

Dated: JANUARY 9th , 2016   X _____
                                                          Anthony Figueroa

STATE OF ____FLORIDA____

COUNTY OF ____FLAGLER____

Sworn to or affirmed and signed before me on January 9, 2016 by ____ANTHONY FIGUEROA____
withIA:FLDL F 260 0128 208 40.

_____
NOTARY PUBLIC or DEPUTY CLERK

_____
[Print, type, or stamp commissioned name of
notary or clerk.]

JUSTIN L. SEEKAMP
MY COMMISSION # FF 239712
EXPIRES: June 11, 2019
Bonded Thru Budget Notary Services

Appendix E: Alessi Affidavit

IN THE CIRCUIT COURT OF THE
SEVENTEENTH JUDICIAL CIRCUIT
IN AND FOR BROWARD COUNTY,
FLORIDA

CASE NO.: CACE 15-000072

EDWARDS, *et al.*,

    Plaintiffs / Counterclaim Defendants,

    v.

DERSHOWITZ,

    Defendant / Counterclaim Plaintiff.

_____/

AFFIDAVIT OF JUAN P. ALESSI
REGARDING KNOWLEDGE OF ALAN M. DERSHOWITZ

A. Introduction

1. My name is Juan P. Alessi. I make this declaration voluntarily and without compensation on personal knowledge concerning Alan Dershowitz and his visits at my former employer Jeffrey Epstein's home in Palm Beach, Florida.

2. I worked for Mr. Epstein from January 1991 to December 2002 as a full-time employee performing maintenance services and then also became the manager for the home on 358 El Brillo Way in Palm Beach, Florida.

3. Since Mr. Epstein was investigated and arrested, I have spoken with police, investigators, and attorneys concerning my time working for Mr. Epstein.

4. On September 8, 2009, I gave a deposition in the case captioned *Jane Doe No. 2 v. Jeffrey Epstein*, Case No. 08-CV-80119 in which I truthfully answered the questions posed by the attorneys. I also gave a sworn statement on November 21, 2005 to

Detective Joseph Recarey of the Palm Beach P.D. during their investigation of Mr. Epstein.

5. I have reviewed the statements that Bradley Edwards and Paul Cassell attribute to me in their papers in the cases against the Government and against Mr. Dershowitz. Because I do not believe they accurately reflect the statements I previously made, I submit this affidavit to have my statements accurately reflected and made clear on the record.

B. Summary of My Knowledge of Massages at Mr. Epstein's Palm Beach Home

6. As I stated in my deposition, a massage was like a treat for all the guests at Mr. Epstein's home. Mr. Epstein usually received his massages in his private suite, but guests would also be given massages in their respective rooms or by the pool area.

7. There were between fifty (50) to one hundred (100) masseuses – mostly women but also some men - who would come to give massages during this time. I provided names of masseuses in my deposition.

8. As I stated in my deposition, I was unaware of any masseuses being under the age of 18. I believed that the females' age ranged from overage to maybe mid-forties. As I stated in my deposition, I received as a gift a massage from a male masseuse at Mr. Epstein's home in Palm Beach.

9. In my deposition, I was asked about cleaning up after massages. I stated that when I cleaned Mr. Epstein's bedroom suite, which included the bathroom of Ms. Maxwell, after massages, I would, on occasion, find vibrators and sex toys. I have specific recollection of finding these items in the sink of Ms. Maxwell's bathroom. I did not state or imply that vibrators or sex toys were found after massages in other rooms used by guests because that was not the case. Guests having massages did not have

2

massages in Mr. Epstein's private bedroom suite. This area was private and off-limits to guests, which I explained to the lawyers during my deposition. As I said in my deposition, massage tables were located in almost every room, including guest rooms and by the pool. I never found, and never heard anyone in the house finding, a vibrator or a sex toy in the same room where any guest, including Alan Dershowitz, had a massage.

10. The following statement made by Virginia Roberts's attorneys in a filing on January 21, 2015 is not accurate and is a misrepresentation of what I said in my deposition: "The private, upstairs room where Dershowitz got his 'massages' was one that contained a lot of vibrators – Maxwell had 'a laundry basket . . . full of those toys' in that room."

C. Summary of My Interaction with Alan M. Dershowitz

11. During the approximate thirteen years I worked for Mr. Epstein, I believe I saw Mr. Dershowitz visit Mr. Epstein's Palm Beach home approximately four or five times a year. I recall driving him to the airport on multiple occasions.

12. At the time, I understood that Mr. Dershowitz was a famous lawyer. His visits to the house would typically involve a group of intellectuals or business men in social, but professional type gatherings.

13. I can recall that Mr. Dershowitz had a massage on at least one occasion during a visit to Mr. Epstein's home in Palm Beach (although I cannot recall that Mr. Dershowitz received a massage on more than one occasion). I do not recall Mr. Dershowitz being massaged by anyone who I thought was less than 18 years old. I have no reason to doubt Mr. Dershowitz's statement that this massage was done by a woman named Olga who was in her forties. In fact, I do remember a masseuse named Olga that

3

lived in Palm Beach, though I do not know her last name. As I have said, I never saw Mr. Dershowitz around young girls. I have also explained that there were masseuses, both male and female, that were in their mid-forties.

14. I never saw Mr. Dershowitz do anything improper or be present while anyone else was being improper.

15. Before asking me about Jeffrey Epstein speaking to celebrities at the house, the attorney for "Jane Doe 102" asked me about Jean Luc Brunel, Mark Epstein, Daniel Estes, Matt Groening, and Leslie Wexner. I then listed Senator Mitchell, Prince Andrew, Princess Sarah Ferguson, Miss Yugoslavia, Miss Germany, Alan Dershowitz, Princess Diana's secretary with her children, Mr. Trump, Mr. Robert Kennedy, Jr., Frederik Fekkai, and a couple Noble prize winners as celebrities that I had seen while working for Mr. Epstein. I also mentioned a reunion of Nobel prize winners that was held at the house, and that I met President Clinton at Mr. Epstein's plane the last month that I was working for Mr. Epstein.

C. Summary of My Interaction with Virginia Roberts

16. The first time I saw Virginia Roberts was at Mar-a-Lago where I believed she worked in the spa. I only recall seeing Virginia Roberts come to Mr. Epstein's house during the last year that I worked for Mr. Epstein. During this time, I believe she visited Mr. Epstein's home in Palm Beach two or three times a week.

17. I never saw any photographs of Virginia Roberts in Mr. Epstein's house. I was shown a photo of Virginia Roberts during my deposition, and I recognized the woman in the photo as Virginia Roberts.

18. As I stated in my deposition, I am not sure whether Virginia Roberts came to the house when Prince Andrew was there.

4

19. I was never asked by any attorneys if Virginia Roberts came to the house when Mr.
Dershowitz was there. If I had been asked, I would have answered that I never saw
Virginia Roberts at the house when Mr. Dershowitz was there.

20. The following statement made by Virginia Roberts's attorneys and their own attorney
in a filing on December 4, 2015 is not accurate and is a misrepresentation of what I
said in my deposition: "Alessi was able to identify a photograph of Ms. Giuffre as
someone who was at the mansion as the same time as Dershowitz."

21. As far as I can recall, since I gave my deposition in 2009, I have never been asked by
Brad Edwards or Paul Cassell about my knowledge regarding Virginia Roberts or
Alan Dershowitz or about my 2009 deposition testimony.

**I understand that I am swearing or affirming under oath to the truthfulness of the
claims made in this affidavit and that the punishment for knowingly making a false
statement includes fines and/or imprisonment.**

Dated: January 13, 2016

STATE OF   _FLORIDA_

COUNTY OF   _PALM BEACH_

Sworn to or affirmed and signed before me on   _JANUARY 13, 2016_
by_____ _JUAN PATRICIO, who provided his driver's
license. ALESSI_

NOTARY PUBLIC or DEPUTY CLERK
LINDA S. COHEN
[Print, type, or stamp commissioned name of
notary or clerk.]

5

Appendix F: FBI Interview of Giuffre Claims, 7/3/2013

FD-302 (Rev. 5-8-10)   -1 of 12-

FEDERAL BUREAU OF INVESTIGATION

Date of entry   07/05/2013

VIRGINIA L. GIUFFRE, maiden name ROBERTS, date of birth
Social Security Account Number   United States Citizen and
Australian Permanent Resident, residence
New South Wales, Australia, 2261 was interviewed at the United States
Consulate in Sydney, Australia. GIUFFRE was advised of the identity of the
interviewing agents and purpose of the interview. Present during the
interview was Federal Bureau of Investigation Special Agent
                                    and via telephone, Assistant   b6
United States Attorney   GIUFFRE provided the   b7C
following information:

GIUFFRE was born in Sacramento, California to parents
                              date of birth   b6
currently resides in   and   date of birth   b7C
                    currently resides in   GIUFFRE moved to Palm
Beach County, Florida with her parents when she was four years old and
returned to California at age 11. She returned to Florida at age 13 and
was placed in a rehabilitation or foster care facility in West Palm Beach,
Florida.

GIUFFRE ran away from the rehabilitation facility when she was
approximately 14 years old, and while living on the streets in Miami,
Florida, she met   b6
                                                                          b7C

Defendant Exhibit
Exhibit No.: *VK 10*
Name: *jh*
Date: *1-16-16*
ⒺESQUIRE

was training GIUFFRE to be an escort
                      gave GIUFFRE a life off of the streets which made her feel

Investigation on 03/17/2011 at Sydney, Australia (In Person)

File # 31E-MM-108062   Date drafted 07/05/2013   b6
                                                                              b7C
by

FD-302a (Rev. 05-08-10)

31E-MM-108062

Continuation of FD-302 of Virginia L. Giuffre _____ , On 03/17/2011 , Page 2 of 12

like she was locked into the relationship.☐ gave GIUFFRE
pharmaceutical drugs toward the end of their relationship.

b6
b7C

GIUFFRE's relationship with☐ended while she was at a private
ranch near Ocala, Florida. GIUFFRE telephonically contacted a childhood
friend,☐ from a telephone at the ranch. GIUFFRE
knew☐from elementary school and called him at the home telephone
of his parents☐GIUFFRE told☐she was
very lonely, and☐asked her why she did not leave
☐GIUFFRE's telephone conversation with☐
☐the recreational vehicle (RV) GIUFFRE was
staying in at the ranch☐did not
strike her☐pack
her belongings and told her she was going to live with another man.

b6
b7C

☐GIUFFRE
felt that she was sent to☐but did not know the
specifics of the arrangement. GIUFFRE engaged in sexual activity with
☐who was described as a white male☐ GIUFFRE stated
☐GIUFFRE stayed with☐LNU for
approximately one or two weeks before the police located her and returned
her to her parents. GIUFFRE was interviewed by a male detective.
GIUFFRE's parents were still married at the time and lived near☐
☐Florida. GIUFFRE believed there was an FBI investigation related to
☐She never saw☐again after

b6
b7C

In approximately June 1998 or 1999, GIUFFRE began working at Donald
Trump's Mar-A-Lago Club in Palm Beach, Florida. GIUFFRE's father☐
☐was able to help her gain
employment as a baby sitter and later as a locker room attendant at the
club. GIUFFRE started studying for her GED and wanted to become a massage
therapist. In August, GIUFFRE was reading an anatomy/massage book and was
approached by☐
☐and help her get her masseuse accreditation.

b6
b7C

GIUFFRE consulted her father about the opportunity and at approximately
5:00 p.m. the same day, her father drove her to a residence at☐

FD-302a (Rev. 05-08-10)

31E-MM-108062

Continuation of FD-302 of Virginia L. Giuffre _____ , On 03/17/2011 , Page 3 of 12

_____ Florida. _____ spoke with GIUFFRE's father and told him
it was a wonderful opportunity for GIUFFRE. GIUFFRE met|_____
_____|also known as|_____|GIUFFRE was led
upstairs|
|_____|

    Once upstairs in|_____
|_____|instructed GIUFFRE to wash her hands prior to
beginning the massage. The massage began|_____|demonstrated massage
techniques to GIUFFRE.

    During the course of the massage,|_____|questioned
GIUFFRE about her past, including her time as a runaway. GIUFFRE was also
asked if she took birth control.

|_____|

    GIUFFRE was given instruction and began kissing|_____
|_____|

    At the conclusion,|_____|instructed GIUFFRE to obtain two warm wash
clothes. One wash cloth was used to clean|_____
second was|_____|to help him relax. GIUFFRE
described|
and GIUFFRE then moved to the steam room and shower where GIUFFRE massaged
|_____|with soap and a loofah in the shower.

    At the conclusion of the shower, GIUFFRE went downstairs and|_____
|_____|
Arrangements were made for GIUFFRE to return to the house the following day
after work. GIUFFRE's cellular phone number was given to|_____|

b6
b7C

b6
b7C

b6
b7C

b6
b7C

b6
b7C

b6
b7C

b6
b7C

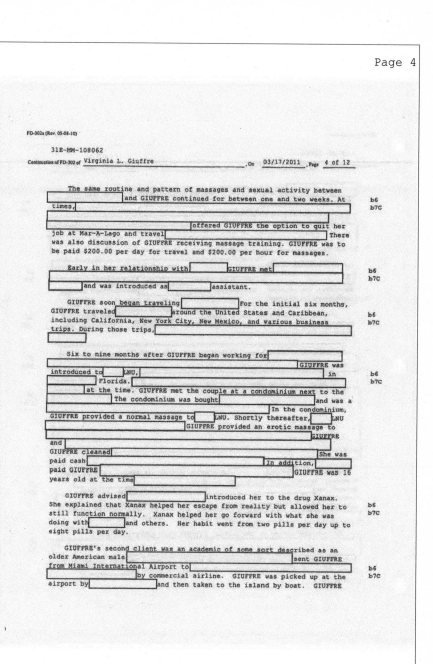

FD-302a (Rev. 05-08-10)

31E-MM-108062

Continuation of FD-302 of Virginia L. Giuffre _____ , On 03/17/2011 , Page 4 of 12

   The same routine and pattern of massages and sexual activity between
_____ and GIUFFRE continued for between one and two weeks. At   b6
times, _____   b7C
_____ offered GIUFFRE the option to quit her
job at Mar-A-Lago and travel _____ There
was also discussion of GIUFFRE receiving massage training. GIUFFRE was to
be paid $200.00 per day for travel and $200.00 per hour for massages.

   Early in her relationship with _____ GIUFFRE met _____   b6
_____ and was introduced as _____ assistant.   b7C

   GIUFFRE soon began traveling _____ For the initial six months,
GIUFFRE traveled _____ around the United States and Caribbean,   b6
including California, New York City, New Mexico, and various business   b7C
trips. During those trips, _____
_____

   Six to nine months after GIUFFRE began working for _____
_____ GIUFFRE was
introduced to _____ LNU, _____ in _____   b6
_____ Florida. _____   b7C
_____ at the time. GIUFFRE met the couple at a condominium next to the
_____ The condominium was bought _____ and was a
_____ In the condominium,
GIUFFRE provided a normal massage to _____ LNU. Shortly thereafter, _____ LNU
_____ GIUFFRE provided an erotic massage to _____
_____ GIUFFRE
and _____
GIUFFRE cleaned _____ She was
paid cash _____ In addition, _____
paid GIUFFRE _____ GIUFFRE was 16
years old at the time. _____

   GIUFFRE advised _____ introduced her to the drug Xanax.
She explained that Xanax helped her escape from reality but allowed her to   b6
still function normally. Xanax helped her go forward with what she was   b7C
doing with _____ and others. Her habit went from two pills per day up to
eight pills per day.

   GIUFFRE's second client was an academic of some sort described as an
older American male _____ sent GIUFFRE
from Miami International Airport to _____   b6
_____ by commercial airline. GIUFFRE was picked up at the   b7C
airport by _____ and then taken to the island by boat. GIUFFRE

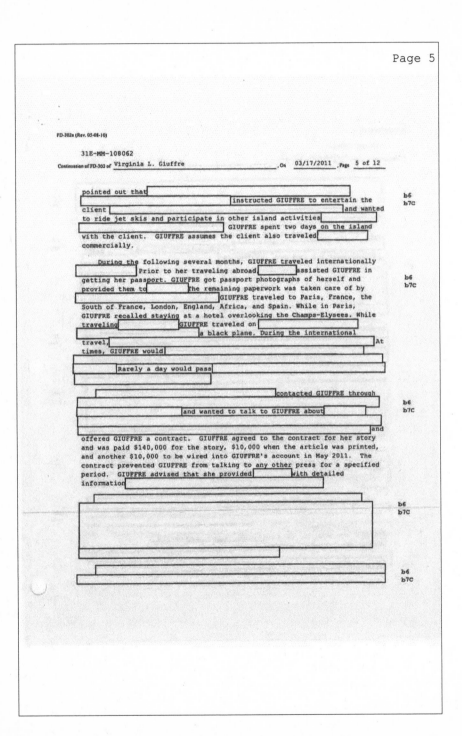

31E-MM-108062
Continuation of FD-302 of Virginia L. Giuffre _____ , On 03/17/2011 , Page 5 of 12

pointed out that _____ instructed GIUFFRE to entertain the
client _____ and wanted
to ride jet skis and participate in other island activities
_____ GIUFFRE spent two days on the island
with the client. GIUFFRE assumes the client also traveled
commercially.

During the following several months, GIUFFRE traveled internationally
_____ Prior to her traveling abroad _____ assisted GIUFFRE in
getting her passport. GIUFFRE got passport photographs of herself and
provided them to _____ The remaining paperwork was taken care of by
_____ GIUFFRE traveled to Paris, France, the
South of France, London, England, Africa, and Spain. While in Paris,
GIUFFRE recalled staying at a hotel overlooking the Champs-Elysees. While
traveling _____ GIUFFRE traveled on _____
_____ a black plane. During the international
travel, _____ At
times, GIUFFRE would _____
_____ Rarely a day would pass _____
_____

_____ contacted GIUFFRE through
_____ and wanted to talk to GIUFFRE about _____
_____ and
offered GIUFFRE a contract. GIUFFRE agreed to the contract for her story
and was paid $140,000 for the story, $10,000 when the article was printed,
and another $10,000 to be wired into GIUFFRE's account in May 2011. The
contract prevented GIUFFRE from talking to any other press for a specified
period. GIUFFRE advised that she provided _____ with detailed
information

b6
b7C

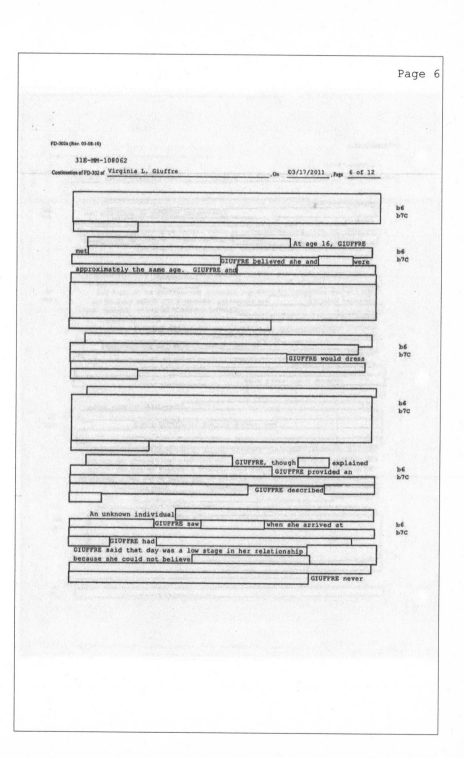

FD-302a (Rev. 05-08-10)

31E-MM-108062

Continuation of FD-302 of Virginia L. Giuffre   , On   03/17/2011 , Page   6 of 12

b6
b7C

At age 16, GIUFFRE
met
GIUFFRE believed she and   were
approximately the same age.   GIUFFRE and

b6
b7C

b6
b7C

GIUFFRE would dress

b6
b7C

b6
b7C

GIUFFRE, though   explained
GIUFFRE provided an

b6
b7C

GIUFFRE described

An unknown individual
GIUFFRE saw   when she arrived at

b6
b7C

GIUFFRE had
GIUFFRE said that day was a low stage in her relationship
because she could not believe

GIUFFRE never

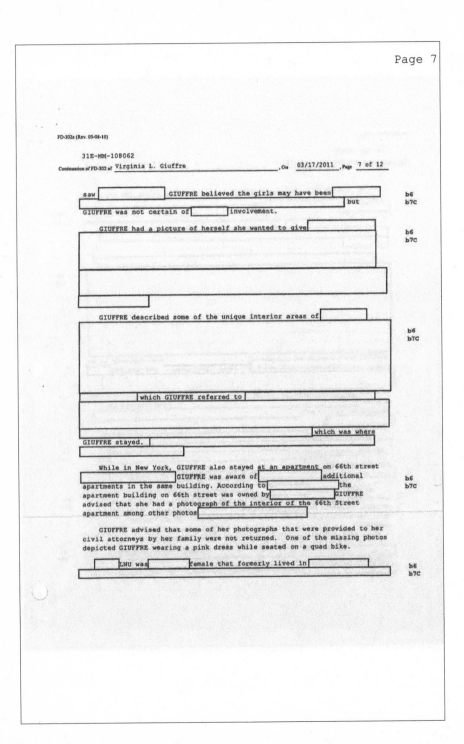

FD-302a (Rev. 05-08-10)

31E-MM-108062

Continuation of FD-302 of Virginia L. Giuffre _____, On 03/17/2011 , Page 7 of 12

saw [   ] GIUFFRE believed the girls may have been [   ]
                                                              but   b6
GIUFFRE was not certain of [   ] involvement.   b7C

    GIUFFRE had a picture of herself she wanted to give [   ]   b6
                                                                       b7C

    GIUFFRE described some of the unique interior areas of [   ]

                                                                       b6
                                                                       b7C

          which GIUFFRE referred to [   ]

                                                                 which was where
GIUFFRE stayed. [   ]

    While in New York, GIUFFRE also stayed at an apartment on 66th street
[   ] GIUFFRE was aware of [   ] additional   b6
apartments in the same building. According to [   ] the   b7C
apartment building on 66th street was owned by [   ] GIUFFRE
advised that she had a photograph of the interior of the 66th street
apartment among other photos [   ]

    GIUFFRE advised that some of her photographs that were provided to her
civil attorneys by her family were not returned. One of the missing photos
depicted GIUFFRE wearing a pink dress while seated on a quad bike.

[   ] LNU was [   ] female that formerly lived in [   ]   b6
                                                                          b7C

FD-302a (Rev. 05-08-10)

31E-MM-108062

Continuation of FD-302 of Virginia L. Giuffre   ,On   03/17/2011 , Page   9 of 12

while there, [   ] approached GIUFFRE in a very excited manner and told
her they had to go shopping to pick out a dress because GIUFFRE would be
dancing with [   ]
       b6
       b7C

    GIUFFRE and [   ] went shopping and purchased makeup, clothing, and a
Burberry bag. The items were purchased with [   ] GIUFFRE
and [   ] returned [   ]
instructed GIUFFRE to get ready. When GIUFFRE came down after getting
ready, she was introduced to [
       b6
       b7C

           GIUFFRE traveled to CLUB TRAMP [   ] GIUFFRE
danced [   ] at CLUB TRAMP [

                                          stayed at CLUB TRAMP
for an hour or hour and a half and drank a couple of cocktails before
returning to [   ] GIUFFRE had not received any direction
from [
                ] After returning to [   ] GIUFFRE
requested [   ] to take a photograph of her [   ] GIUFFRE
advised that she still had the original photograph in her possession and
would provide it to the interviewing agents. GIUFFRE proceeded with [

           Approximately two months later, GIUFFRE met [   ] at
       b6
       b7C

                     GIUFFRE recalled [
           LNU, [

          GIUFFRE recalled [   ] joking about trading GIUFFRE in because
she was getting too old.

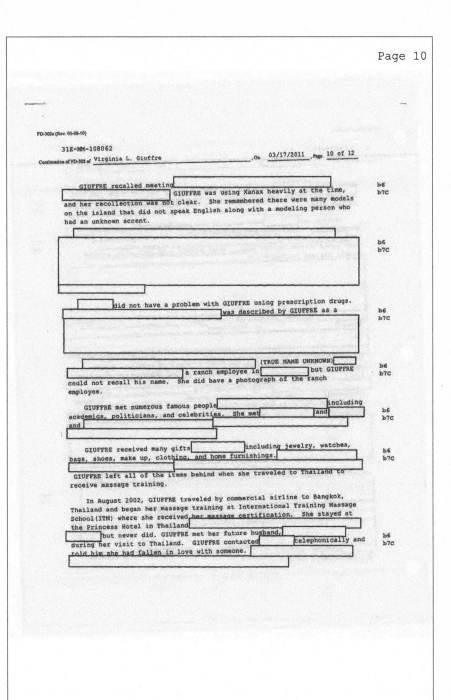

FD-302a (Rev. 05-08-10)

31E-MM-108062

Continuation of FD-302 of Virginia L. Giuffre _____ , On 03/17/2011 , Page 10 of 12

GIUFFRE recalled meeting [   ]
[   ] GIUFFRE was using Xanax heavily at the time,   b6
and her recollection was not clear. She remembered there were many models   b7C
on the island that did not speak English along with a modeling person who
had an unknown accent.

[   ]   b6
                                                                          b7C

[   ] did not have a problem with GIUFFRE using prescription drugs.
[   ] was described by GIUFFRE as a   b6
                                                                          b7C

[   ] (TRUE NAME UNKNOWN) [   ] b6
[   ] a ranch employee in [   ] but GIUFFRE   b7C
could not recall his name. She did have a photograph of the ranch
employee.

GIUFFRE met numerous famous people [   ] including
academics, politicians, and celebrities. She met [   ] and [   ] b6
and [   ]   b7C

GIUFFRE received many gifts [   ] including jewelry, watches,   b6
bags, shoes, make up, clothing, and home furnishings. [   ]   b7C
GIUFFRE left all of the items behind when she traveled to Thailand to
receive massage training.

In August 2002, GIUFFRE traveled by commercial airline to Bangkok,
Thailand and began her massage training at International Training Massage
School(ITM) where she received her massage certification. She stayed at
the Princess Hotel in Thailand [   ]
[   ] but never did. GIUFFRE met her future husband, [   ]   b6
during her visit to Thailand. GIUFFRE contacted [   ] telephonically and   b7C
told him she had fallen in love with someone. [   ]

FD-302a (Rev. 05-08-10)

31E-MM-108062

Continuation of FD-302 of Virginia L. Giuffre   , On 03/17/2011 , Page 11 of 12

GIUFFRE had not heard from [ ]
[ ] GIUFFRE received a
telephone call from [ ] During that call, [ ] stated he was an
FBI agent. He was trying to determine what she knew about [ ]
[ ] She did not tell [ ] anything about her knowledge of
[ ] She also received another telephone call from a
person that indicated he was an FBI agent. She did not tell that
individual anything either. She also received a call from an attorney that
was trying to determine if she had spoken with anyone or was willing to
speak to anyone [ ]
[ ] She
explained that she was receiving telephone calls from people whom she did
not know and that she was uncomfortable telling them anything over the
telephone.

One or two weeks later, an unknown attorney and [ ] contacted
GIUFFRE telephonically. [ ]
[ ]

GIUFFRE was using a cellular telephone belonging to her husband. She
nor her husband could recall the telephone number but advised that the
carrier was OPTUS telephone company.

GIUFFRE reviewed a series of photographs of individuals and identified
the following:

Page 1, number 1, [ ]

Page 1, number 2, [ ] LNU, a.k.a. [ ]

Page 2, number 1, [ ]

Page 2, number 6, [ ]

Page 3, number 2, [ ]

Page 4, number 3, [ ] LNU

Page 4, number 7, [ ]

Page 4, number 8, [ ]

Page 5, number 1, [ ]

GIUFFRE advised that the following were familiar to her, but she could not
recall their names or her association to them:

b6 b7C

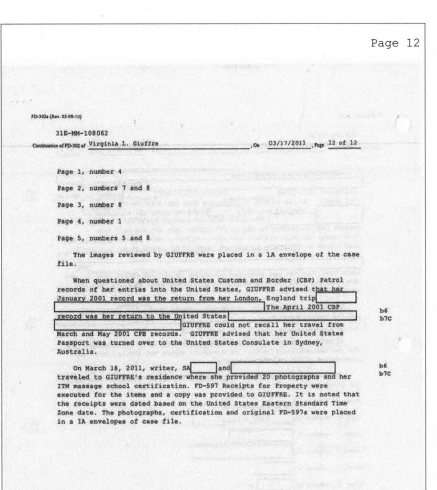

FD-302a (Rev. 05-08-10)

31E-MM-108062

Continuation of FD-302 of Virginia L. Giuffre _____ , On 03/17/2011 , Page 12 of 12

Page 1, number 4

Page 2, numbers 7 and 8

Page 3, number 8

Page 4, number 1

Page 5, numbers 5 and 8

The images reviewed by GIUFFRE were placed in a 1A envelope of the case file.

When questioned about United States Customs and Border (CBP) Patrol records of her entries into the United States, GIUFFRE advised that her January 2001 record was the return from her London, England trip _____. The April 2001 CBP record was her return to the United States _____ GIUFFRE could not recall her travel from March and May 2001 CPB records. GIUFFRE advised that her United States Passport was turned over to the United States Consulate in Sydney, Australia.

On March 18, 2011, writer, SA _____ and _____ traveled to GIUFFRE's residence where she provided 20 photographs and her ITM massage school certification. FD-597 Receipts for Property were executed for the items and a copy was provided to GIUFFRE. It is noted that the receipts were dated based on the United States Eastern Standard Time Zone date. The photographs, certification and original FD-597s were placed in a 1A envelopes of case file.

b6
b7C

b6
b7C

[This interview tracks what Giuffre wrote in her manuscript. We are seeking to have the interview unredacted.]

APPENDIX G: EXCERPTS FROM THE MEMOIRS OF VIRGINIA ROBERTS GIUFFRE

Every single person in this shared world together has a unique story of his or her own to tell, this one is mine.

I spent my sweet 16th birthday on his island in the Caribbean next to "St. James Isle" he liked to call it "Little St. Jeff's", his ego was as enormous as his appetite for fornicating. I was given a birthday cake and a new collection of designer make-up from London.

Instead I would be going to the exclusive hotel in Palm Beach tonight, The Breaker's, where I would be meeting my first ever clients. Only told their first names I was given some instructions and the address where to meet Glen and Eva.

I was having intercourse with this man that was so comfortable doing all of this while his pregnant wife and children slept in the room beside us. When he had climaxed, we both got up and dressed and he paid me a large tip even though Jeffrey would be the one to actually pay me for my time spent there.

Two weeks later, as if Jeffrey was trying to lighten my spirits, he told me I would be going to his island to meet a new client He is a Harvard Professor, named Stephen ██████ . I would be spending two days with him showing him around the island, dining with him, and treating him to a massage whenever he wanted. Without Jeffrey even verbalizing the need to have sex with him, he told me to keep him happy like I had my first client.

We had a guest in the car, and apparently we had already been introduced, but I couldn't even remember his name in the first five minutes of our meeting again. He was the hotel owner of some large chain in America called "Hilton".

Holding back any composure now, he was going extremely wild ravishing at my body trying to tear off my panties like a hungered wild animal. After all of the champagne I had drunk that night it gave me the nerve that I needed to know exactly how to handle perverts like this one, who had been no different from every other shmuck in my life, and I quickly shut him up with a blowjob lasting no longer than two terrible minutes.

At the island, Ghislane had just recently obtained her helicopter pilot's license and wanted to get some practice airtime and flew Jeffrey and I to St. John where we picked up Alexandria Cousteau, the grand daughter to the inventor of the scuba tank and underwater explorer Jack Cousteau. Ghislane was out to set us affright in the air, but it was all talk, she was actually an impressive pilot. Still a daredevil though, she got her kicks out of hearing us fret on the earmuffs intercom's. Jeffrey made it clear that Alexandria was a guest when I was told to adhere to her if she wanted a massage, which I obliged her with several times during our first meeting. It was Jeffrey who instigated that her and I reenact as lovers in lesbian acts of foreplay and penetration.

It was during those intellectual gatherings that my body was also put on the banquet menu but this time for a powerful senator George Mitchell and another prominent Nobel-Prize winning scientist who's name would be mentioned but for all the life of me can no longer remember. They would be only some of the recognizable figures of the high society that became added to my list of clientele, of course being introduced to for a lot more than just a client of massage.

Prince Andrew is described in the next excerpt.

Trying to do the best of my youthfulness to try and act seductive, I gradually began to strip off my clothing, piece by piece. Giving him time to savor the moment to come. He loved every second of it as I went over to where he was waiting and watching, then began to undress him at a much quicker pace. We kissed and touched each other before submersing into the hot water, where we both continued to reenact foreplay. He was adorning my young body, particularly my feet, caressing my toes and licking my arches. That was definitely a first for me and I couldn't help but laugh, I hoped he didn't expect the same treatment back. Through my recent experiences with Rena, I drew a line with extreme fetishes, especially ones that would involve my tongue and feet in the same sentence. It wasn't hard to get him wound up to the point where he just wanted to have the rest of me so we dried off from the cold and retired to my bedchambers for the longest ten minutes of my life. Moments later and without any real emotional attachment, he burst in ecstasy, leaving me to my own feelings of dismay.

Then I met Al Gore and his lovely wife during
one of those many weekends away in the Caribbean. I was blown away
by the amount of attention Al doted on his wife, it was so sweet to watch.
They sat next to each other at the dinner table gazing into one another's
eyes having an intimate conversation between them. Among the many
guests visiting that night and many of them young beautiful women, not
once did Al's eye's stray elsewhere, to them they were the only ones
there. He was up for a presidential election that year and he definitely had
my vote. Anyone that could show that much devotion and passion
towards his loved ones could have the same devotion towards running a
country, or at least I thought so. He only left his wife's side to have a
walk down to the beach with the host of the weekend, Jeffrey. The
weather was still warm in the evening when I decided to break away from
the idle chat around the table and take a stroll too.

The next big dinner party on the island had another significant guest
appearance being, the one and only, Bill Clinton. He is the only president
in the world to be dismissed from his role as a world leader because he
was caught with his trousers around his ankles and had the stain to prove
it. Publicly humiliating his wife and himself he retired from his title but
not from his lifestyle. This wasn't a big party as such, only a few of us
eating at the diner table. There was Jeffrey at the head of it all, as always.
On the left side was Emmy, Ghislane and I. Sitting across the table from
us was Bill with two lovely girls who were visiting from New York.
Bill's wife, Hillary's absence from the night made it easy for his apparent
provocative cheeky side to come out. Teasing the girls on either side of
him with playful pokes and brassy comments, there was no modesty
between any of them. We all finished our meals and scattered in our own
different directions.

Jeffrey's business was running well from the looks of his attentiveness
the office he owned in the Upper East Side of Manhattan. Alan
Dershowitz, his colleague in finances and personal solicitor, a bird of the
same feather, I had seen hanging around the island and Jeffrey's
Manhattan mansion, more and more these days. Alan's taste for the
young and beautiful was a bias for a blooming business relationship
between him and Jeffrey. After an explicit session of Jeffrey's vulgar
pilgrimage into my body, we were interrupted by a knock at the door by
Jeffrey's good friend, Alan. I wrapped myself up in Jeffrey's pink bed
sheets, which is the color preference he chose to sleep in because it
reminded him of the same color of his own words "Pussy", and covered

my face from the unexpected intrusion. Jeffrey got up and wrapped a towel around his loins and answered the door completely calm. Opening the bedroom door and letting Alan inside they began to converse about business immediately, right in front of me. Jeffrey started to tell Alan what needed to be done while he jostled some notes down quickly. I peeked my head from underneath the covers thinking they were too wrapped up in their work to notice me get up and dressed, and Jeffrey turned back to me and told me to just stay there this would only take a second. Going back to Alan he turned his focus back into work and hustled out a few more orders before letting Alan out of the door and returning his attention to me.

"Sorry about that, work never stops and neither will the money coming in. How else am I going to make a million dollars while I'm sleeping?"

APPENDIX H: MEMO AFTER CONVERSATION WITH *NEW YORK POST* REPORTER, WITH CONTEMPORANEOUS HANDWRITTEN CHANGES AND ADDITIONS

Memo my legal team
From Alan Dershowitz
[dictated at] 2:59 p.m. Friday, February 9, 2018

[Jonathan Plotzik]

I was having lunch at the Betsy Ross hotel in Miami Beach with ~~Joel Plotnik~~ his son Zack and a journalist named Peter Goodwin when the phone ran just before 2 pm. It was Maureen Callahan a reporter for the New York Post who I had previously emailed and tried to call. We discussed a potential story and I then asked her if she remembered a woman named Sarah Ransom she said that she did remember getting emails and calls from ~~her~~ *[Ransom]* in which she was accusing everyone under the sun of having sex with her. She specifically said that she had videos of the Clintons and Donald Trump in sexually compromising situations. She said that she had asked Ransom for the videos or any other evidence *and that she could not back up* anything she said. I asked Callahan why she didn't run with the story. She laughed and said: "It was too good to be true." She again repeated that she had no evidence or back up despite the claims in the emails that Ransom had videos and eyewitnesses. Her story was too fantastic and not credible and Ransom herself did not seem to be a credible person. Callahan said that the New York Post would never publish ~~anything~~ this kind of accusation. Callahan said that she didn't call Ransom a liar, but she certainly made it clear that she could not publish this kind accusation. I would never run accusations against anybody public or private, based on the kind of non-credible information Ransom provided. "

[photographs and other evidence]

[including with underage girls]

[Ransom]

[(from R)]

I asked Callahan if any of the conversations or emails were off the record, for background or in any other way confidential. Callahan said absolutely not. Ransom wanted me to publish everything she sent me, so nothing was off the record.

[because she couldn't be sure whether she was fantasizing or deliberately lying]

I asked her if she would send me copies of the emails and she had no problem doing so because nothing was off the record or confidential, but that she would have to check with higher ups at the post because "Technically the emails are the property of the Post." She said she would get back to me. She then asked me why I was interested and I told her she had made accusations against me. Callahan responded, "Why would she do that? She never accused you when she spoke or wrote to me. She accused almost ~~every~~ other well-known ~~person~~ but she never accused you."

[shortly after completing the call, I wrote a brief note to my lawyers and then spoke to them about the call]

Appendix I: Public Statements with Settlement, Including by Former FBI Director Louis Freeh and Documents Related to Freeh Investigation

FOR IMMEDIATE RELEASE **Contact:** Richard A. Simpson, RSimpson@wileyrein.com
April 8, 2016

Lawyers Acknowledge Mistake In Filing Sexual Misconduct Charges Against Professor Dershowitz

Professor Alan M. Dershowitz released the following statement regarding resolution of the case styled *Bradley Edwards, et al. v. Alan M. Dershowitz*, Case No. CACE 15-000072 (Cir. Ct., Broward Cnty., Fla.).

STATEMENT OF ALAN M. DERSHOWITZ

I am pleased that the litigation has concluded and I am gratified by the Joint Statement issued today by Jeffrey E. Streitfeld on behalf of the parties, in which "Edwards and Cassell acknowledge that it was a mistake to have filed sexual misconduct accusations against Dershowitz and the sexual misconduct accusations made in all public filings (including all exhibits) are hereby withdrawn." Mr. Streitfeld's announcement and the Joint Statement are copied below.

ANNOUNCEMENT BY JEFFREY E. STREITFELD, FLORIDA SUPREME COURT CERTIFIED CIRCUIT CIVIL MEDIATOR (Streitfeldlaw.com)

It is my pleasure to report that Bradley J. Edwards, Paul G. Cassell, and Alan M. Dershowitz have resolved their disputes and have agreed to settle the claims raised in an action pending in the Broward County, Florida Circuit Court. Since being appointed by Circuit Court Judge Thomas Lynch IV last fall, it has been a privilege to act as the mediator and assist the parties and their counsel toward this agreed resolution. I want to extend my appreciation for the professionalism exhibited by the parties and their counsel with whom I worked directly: Jack Scarola, Rick Simpson, Tom Scott, and Ken Sweder. As part of their agreement, the parties have issued the attached Joint Statement.

JOINT STATEMENT OF BRAD EDWARDS, PAUL CASSELL AND ALAN DERSHOWITZ REGARDING SETTLEMENT

Brad Edwards, Paul Cassell and Alan Dershowitz have today settled their pending defamation claims in which Edwards and Cassell sued Dershowitz and Dershowitz counterclaimed against Edwards and Cassell. The case was about Dershowitz's public claims that Edwards and Cassell, as the attorneys for Virginia Roberts, had failed to perform the necessary due diligence before filing the allegations of their client, not whether the acts of alleged misconduct in fact occurred. Edwards and Cassell vigorously denied the contention that they had acted improperly and asserted that it defamed them. Dershowitz countersued Edwards and Cassell, alleging they had falsely accused him of sexual contact with Roberts—a claim he vigorously denied and that Dershowitz asserted defamed him. Edwards and Cassell maintain that they filed their client's allegations in good faith and performed the necessary due diligence to do so, and have produced documents detailing those efforts. Dershowitz completely denies any such misconduct, while not disputing Roberts's statements that the underlying alleged misconduct may have occurred with someone else. Dershowitz has produced travel and other records for the relevant times which he relies on to establish that he could not have been present when the alleged misconduct occurred. He has also produced other evidence that he relies upon to refute the credibility of the allegations against him.

The parties believe it is time to take advantage of the new information that has come to light on both sides during the litigation and put these matters behind them.

Given the events that have transpired since the filing of the documents in the federal court and in this action in which Dershowitz was accused of sexual misconduct, including the court order striking the allegations in the federal court filings, and the records and other documents produced by the parties, Edwards and Cassell acknowledge that it was a mistake to have filed sexual misconduct accusations against Dershowitz; and the sexual misconduct accusations made in all public filings (including all exhibits) are hereby withdrawn. Dershowitz also withdraws his accusations that Edwards and Cassell acted unethically.

Neither Edwards, Cassell, nor Dershowitz have any intention of repeating the allegations against one another.

# # # #

Editor's note: Wiley Rein LLP represents Alan M. Dershowitz in this matter.

FOR IMMEDIATE RELEASE   Contact: Richard A. Simpson, RSimpson@wileyrein.com
April 8, 2016

INVESTIGATION BY FORMER FBI DIRECTOR LOUIS FREEH CONCLUDES THAT THE TOTALITY OF THE EVIDENCE REFUTES ALLEGATIONS MADE AGAINST PROFESSOR DERSHOWITZ

Professor Alan M. Dershowitz today issued the following statement regarding the results of the independent investigation conducted by former FBI Director Louis Freeh of sexual misconduct allegations made against Prof. Dershowitz.

STATEMENT OF PROFESSOR ALAN M. DERSHOWITZ

I am gratified by the statement by former federal judge and former FBI Director Louis Freeh set forth below. Following his independent investigation of the sexual misconduct accusations made against me, it concludes that in Judge Freeh's professional opinion, "The totality of the evidence found during the investigation refutes the allegations made against Professor Dershowitz."

STATEMENT OF LOUIS J. FREEH

Over the past several months, an independent investigation was conducted, under my supervision, by former senior federal law enforcement officials. We interviewed many witnesses and reviewed thousands of pages of documentary evidence. Our investigation found no evidence to support the accusations of sexual misconduct against Professor Dershowitz. In fact, in several instances, the evidence directly contradicted the accusations made against him.

In my opinion, the totality of the evidence found during the investigation refutes the allegations made against Professor Dershowitz.

# # # #

Editor's note: Wiley Rein LLP represents Alan M. Dershowitz.

March 9, 2019

To Whom It May Concern:

In 2015, Professor Alan Dershowitz retained Freeh Group International Solutions, LLC ("FGIS") to conduct an independent investigation into allegations of sexual misconduct that had been made against him by Ms. Virginia Roberts. Ms. Roberts also made allegations against others, including former President William Clinton.

During the course of our investigation, personnel from FGIS, including a former senior prosecutor and investigator from the U.S. Department of Justice with more than a half century of collective experience conducting criminal investigations, carefully examined thousands of pages of documentary evidence, much of which Professor Dershowitz supplied to us; sought to reconstruct events in New York City, Palm Beach, Little St. James Island, a ranch in New Mexico, and on a private aircraft; and, identified and interviewed many witnesses who were able to provide relevant details regarding Ms. Roberts' allegations. In our opinion, the totality of the evidence found during the investigation refutes the allegations made against Professor Dershowitz.

In addition, FGIS made a Freedom of Information Act ("FOIA") request to the U.S. Secret Service ("USSS") for "any and all gift logs, travel records, itineraries, reports and other records for USSS personnel traveling with former President William Clinton to Little St. James Island." This was done in an effort to determine whether former President Clinton had been there as Ms. Roberts alleged.

On January 16, 2016, the official in charge of the USSS's FOIA/PA Office replied by letter that the "USSS has conducted a reasonable search for responsive records" and "from a review of USSS main indices, that there are no records pertaining to your request that are referenced in these indices." Thus, the conclusion that can be drawn that, contrary to Ms. Roberts' allegation, former President Clinton did not in fact travel to, nor was he present on, Little St. James Island between January 1, 2001 and January 1, 2003. The FOIA results not only directly impeach Ms. Roberts' specific allegations against Professor Dershowitz, but in our opinion completely undermine her credibility. Together with our other factual findings and conclusions, it is our opinion that all of these allegations against him were made without any basis.

At the conclusion of our investigation, which was conducted under the supervision of FGIS Chairman Louis J. Freeh, FGIS concluded that we "found no evidence to support the accusations of sexual misconduct against Professor Dershowitz. In fact, in several instances, the evidence directly contradicted the accusations made against him."

We stand by our investigation and that conclusion.

Very truly yours,

James R. Bucknam
President and Chief Executive Officer

Appendix J: Excerpt from Pottinger Affidavit

9. In the fall of 2014, I asked Mr. Boies if his firm represented, or if he knew, Mr. Leslie Wexner. I told him that in the course of investigating facts related to Mr. Epstein's sex trafficking, Mr. Wexner had been identified as a close business associate and personal friend of Mr. Epstein. I told Mr. Boies that there were assertions that Mr. Wexner had permitted Mr. Epstein to use, and entertain on, Mr. Wexner's Yacht, and that Mr. Wexner was alleged to have had sex with one or more of Mr. Epstein's girls, including Ms. Giuffre.

10. Mr. Boies told me that his firm did not represent Mr. Wexner or his companies, but that he had met Mr. Wexner at one or more dinner parties. Mr. Boies cautioned that before any assertions by Ms. Giuffre about Mr. Wexner were made, the facts should be thoroughly investigated and Mr. Wexner should be given a chance to address the assertions she was making about him. I agreed and asked Mr. Boies if BSF would undertake that investigation. Mr. Boies said he would ask BSF lawyers in Florida to help.

11. I know that Mr. Wexner was initially contacted for a discussion with him and/or his counsel in December 2014 by Mr. Steve Zack, the head of BSF's Miami office and the former President of the Florida Bar and of the American Bar Association. I also know that Messrs. Zack, Boies, and one or more other lawyers at BSF subsequently spoke with counsel for Mr. Wexner.

APPENDIX K: CHURCHER EMAILS (IN REVERSE ORDER)

Hi Jarred

Hopefully you have Virginia's book pitch by now.

She has some amazing names which she can share with you in confidence and I think she also has a human interest story that could appeal to the Oprah/female set as well as the Wall Streeters who follow Epstein – a hedge fund king.

Here are a few of our stories about Virginia, plus some examples of the massive US and other international media pickup. Vanity Fair are doing a piece I believe in their August issue. The FBI have reopened the Epstein case due to Virginia's revelations. I also am attaching a link to a NY Magazine profile of Epstein.....written before his world combusted. The FBI believe he was essentially running a private – and mobile – brothel for some of the world's richest and most influential men.

He got off the first time round after retaining Kenneth Starr (who witchhunted Bill Clinton) and Alan Dershowitz (von Bulow's appeal lawyer, who inspired the movie Reversal of Fortune). The US Justice Dept is investigating corruption allegations against at least one prosecutor involved in the case.

Best regards,

Sharon

To:	Sharon.Churcher@mailonsunday.co.uk[▓▓▓▓▓▓▓▓▓▓▓▓]
From:	Virginia Giuffre
Sent:	Thur 5/12/2011 2:21:43 AM
Importance:	Normal
Subject:	Re: Good News!!
Received:	Thur 5/12/2011 2:21:43 AM

Thanks again Shazza, I'm bringing down the house with this book!!!
xoxo Jenna

--- On Wed, 11/5/11, Sharon.Churcher@mailonsunday.co.uk *<Sharon.Churcher@mailonsunday.co.uk>* wrote:

From: Sharon.Churcher@mailonsunday.co.uk < ▓▓▓▓▓▓▓▓▓▓▓▓▓▓▓ >
Subject: Re: Good News!!
To: "Virginia Giuffre" <robiejennag@y7mail.com>
Received: Wednesday, 11 May, 2011, 4:17 PM

Don't forget Alan Dershowitz...JE's buddy and lawyer..good name for your pitch as he repped Claus von Bulow and a movie was made about that case...title was Reversal of Fortune. We all suspect Alan is a pedo and tho no proof of that, you probably met him when he was hanging put w JE

```
|-----------------------------------------------------------------|
|Hi Sharon,                                    |
|                                         |
|Hello gorgeous, I hope this message comes to you on a bright, sunny day!!!|
|I took your advice about what to offer Sandra and she accepted. Were  |
|drawing up a contract through her agent right now and getting busy to meet|
|my deadline. Just wondering if you have any information on you from when |
|you and I were doing interviews about the J.E story. I wanted to put the |
|names of some of these assholes, oops, I meant to say, pedo's, that J.E  |
|sent me to. With everything going on my brain feels like mush and it would|
|be a great deal of help!                         |
|Having fun sweetie?                           |
|                                         |
|Thanks,                                     |
|Jenna                                      |
|-----------------------------------------------------------------|
```

APPENDIX L: TRAVEL DOCUMENT PAGES

Date	Location	AD Agenda	CC Agenda	Financial Records: Restaurants	Financial Records: Merchants	Financial Records: Travel	Phone Logs***	Class Schedule	Misc. Records	Archival Records
					December 2001					
9 (Sun)	New York-Boston	New York, CT TV (front of book)/ 4: Judges?/ supplemental- Ethyl Rosenberg? / Channukah?	Dershowitz party	Credit Card: 435600500047062 6 (US Airways Dividend Miles visa): Westwood Mass.			[redacted]			
10	Cambridge	Basketball		Fugakyu, Brookline Mass. (AmEx monthly statement 2001-10)	Credit Card: 435600500047062 6 (US Airways Dividend Miles visa): Brookline Mass.		[redacted]			CNN live, guest appearance form Boston (Brooklyn College Archives, Video Records, TV interviews, Box 9)
11	Cambridge	Cambridge/ students 6:30/ letter to Clinton/ Forward	Alan's class for dinner at 6:30				[redacted]	Class: Criminal Law 1, 11:50-1:20		
12	Cambridge	Cambridge/ 4:30 Chapman					[redacted]		CNN "Crossfire," "Live with Paula Zahn," Guest appearance from Boston	
13	Cambridge	Cambridge/ Book for Review/ Last Class?					[redacted]			
14	Cambridge	Cambridge/ Buch. 5:30-7:30/ 10:30 Baden			Medical Receipt, Massachusetts General Physicians Organization Inc. acct. no. 1903318, Alan Dershowitz, Office OP. Visit, Est. Pt., Mr. Baden Md.		[redacted]			
15	Cambridge	Wexner/ Send books to law records	Sharon + David concerts/ 6:00 Radius	Radius, Boston (AmEx monthly statement 2001-11)			[redacted]			
16 (Sun)	Cambridge		3 Penny Opera at 2:00 at Huntington Theater	Chau Chow City Inc., Boston (AmEx monthly statement 2001-11)			[redacted]			

*** These are phone calls that identify numbers and locations. They have been redacted to protect privacy.

November 2001

November

Date	Location	AD Agenda	CC Agenda	Financial Records: Restaurants	Financial Records: Merchants	Financial Records: Travel	Phone Logs	Class Schedule	Misc. Records	Archival Records
1	Cambridge-New York	New York- St. Louis, speech, CT TV (front of book)/ Train to New York					████			
2	New York	New York- St. Louis, speech, CT TV (front of book)/ New York/ CT TV/ Lunch 6: Barak		Rosa Mexicano, Fat Free Food, New York (AmEx monthly statement 2001-9)	Sussex Wine/ Spirit, Cardsnyc, New York (AmEx monthly statement 2001-9)		████			
3	New York	New York (book 3)/ 1:30 Opera/ Louis Heller	CC to New York	Shun Lee; Woe Lae Oak New York (AmEx monthly statement 2001-9)	Museum of AM, New York (AmEx monthly statement 2001-9)		████			
4 (Sun)	New York-St. Louis- Boston	New York- St. Louis, speech, CT TV (front of book)/ St. Louis/ 4:30 St. Louis	AD to St. Louis			Garber's Travel, ticket from New York to St. Louis to Boston on American Airlines (AmEx monthly statement 2001-9)	████			Opening Night of St. Louis Jewish Book Festival, Q&A (Brooklyn College Records, Audio Records, Box 7)
5	Cambridge	New York- St. Louis, speech, CT TV (front of book)/ 1: Rosslyn/ Lehman Hill		Fugakyu, Brookline Mass. (AmEx monthly statement 2001-9)	Gap #2242, Brookline Mass. (AmEx monthly statement 2001-9)		████			Appearance on Court TV as guest from Cambridge (Brooklyn College Archives, Video Records, TV interviews, Box 8)
6	Cambridge	Cambridge/ Library- Time?/ Call Bershman/ 9:30 Prep Exam/ Play						Class: Criminal Law 1, 11:50-1:20		
7	Cambridge	Cambridge	AD public library night/ Bball Michael Jordan							
8	Cambridge	Play	7:30 at Market Theater, reservations for 2 under Cohen							
9	Cambridge	Basketball	6:30 Dinner/ Blue Room							

Date	Location	AD Agenda	CC Agenda	Financial Records: Restaurants	Financial Records: Merchants	Financial Records: Travel	Phone Logs	Class Schedule	Misc. Records	Archival Records
					January 2001					
22	New York	Paper/ Fly/ Baden/ 1: Eisetricht/ 8: Opera		Café C3, New York (AmEx monthly statement 2001-A)						CT TV Appearance as host, (Brooklyn College Archives, Video Records, TV interviews, Box 3)
23	New York	Ratner/ 6: Brief Faculty								
24	New York	10: Howard/ 12: Who-Donach		Warehouse Wine and Spirit, New York (AmEx monthly statement 2001-A)	Coconuts #0140, Dryden Gallery, New York (AmEx monthly statement 2001-A)					
25	New York	12: Gotlieb: Paul Verbeil/ 2:15, 12 E 12 St.	American Rhapsody, 8 PM: 4 tickets							
26	New York	CT TV	6:45 Savoy 70 Prince St./ 5:30 H. arrive at hotel	Savoy Restaurant, Jean-Georges Restaurant, New York (AmEx monthly statement 2001-A)						
27	New York	Ella Birthday/ 6: 14 Elizabeth st., Canal & Bayard		Woe Lae Oak, New York (AmEx monthly statement 2001-A)	Design & Comfort Soho, New York (AmEx monthly statement 2001-A)					
28 (Sun)	New York	Ken Sweder	Hiershhorns leave at 3:00/ Gerry Sweder party 4:30							
29	New York	Rick/ Magic-Basketball		ACME bar & Grill, New York (AmEx monthly statement 2001-A)						
30	New York	4-6 CT TV	Chelsea—AD, LRSH mathnite, 6:30-8:00/ AD lunch Pelea Gallery							CT TV Appearance as host (Brooklyn College Archives. Video Records, TV interviews, Box 3)/ Geraldo Rivera Live, guest appearance from New York (Brooklyn College Archives, Video Records, TV interviews, Box 7)

January 2001

Date	Location	AD Agenda	CC Agenda	Financial Records: Restaurants	Financial Records: Merchants	Financial Records: Travel	Phone Logs	Class Schedule	Misc. Records	Archival Records
12	New York	New York (2000/4)/ 1: crime, 2: CT TV		Shun Lee West, New York (AmEx year end statement 2001)	Louis Martin Jeweler, New York (AmEx year end statement 2001)		██████			Appearance on CT TV as Host (Brooklyn College Archives, Video interviews, Box 3 & Box 6)
13	Newark-VA. Beach/Norfolk	Norfolk, Virginia Beach (front of book)/ VA Beach			The Museum Co #82, Newark NJ (AmEx monthly statement 2001-A)		██████			
14 (Sun)	VA. Beach /Norfolk- Newark	Norfolk, Virginia Beach (front of book)/ Atl. City			VA Beach Resort Hotel, VA. (Amex monthly statement 2001-A)	Continental Airlines ticket from Norfolk Va. To Newark (AmEx monthly statement 2001-A)	██████			
15	New York	Groldo/ Pint.					██████			
16	Lebanon Pa.	DuPont	AD in Philadelphia		Faber Coe & Gregg, Philadelphia Pa. (AmEx monthly statement 2001-A)		██████			
17	New York	Rosen	CC Calendar: Robert Rosen, 15 W. 16th Street, Event for Book, benefit dinner							
18	New York	Fletcher, 8: Dany (2001/1)/ New York (2000/4)/ Fletcher/ 8: Dance event 8PM, Rolnick	7PM Rolnicks, Kellerman dinner							
19	New York	New York (2000/4)/ CT TV. Opera/ Rolnick (2001/1)	Aida at 7:00							Appearance on CT TV as host (Brooklyn College Archives, Video Records, TV interviews, Box 6)
20	New York	New York (2000/4)		March, New York (AmEx monthly statement 2001-A)						
21 (Sun)	New York (2000/4)	11-1 Sacks/ 4 Concert/ Rolnick	Rolnick/ Ellisen, 6:30 buffet + cocktails at 812.5th Avenue							

APPENDIX M: *DAILY MAIL* ARTICLE EXCERPT [MARCH 5TH, 2011]

On one occasion, she adds, Epstein did invite two young brunettes to a dinner which he gave on his Caribbean island for Mr Clinton shortly after he left office. But, as far as she knows, the ex-President did not take the bait.

'I'd have been about 17 at the time,' she says. 'I flew to the Caribbean with Jeffrey and then Ghislaine Maxwell went to pick up Bill in a huge black helicopter that Jeffrey had bought her.

'She'd always wanted to fly and Jeffrey paid for her to take lessons, and I remember she was very excited because she got her licence around the first year we met.

'I used to get frightened flying with her but Bill had the Secret Service with him and I remember him talking about what a good job she did.

. . .

'We all dined together that night. Jeffrey was at the head of the table. Bill was at his left. I sat across from him. Emmy Tayler, Ghislaine's blonde British assistant, sat at my right.

'Ghislaine was at Bill's left and at the left of Ghislaine there were two olive-skinned brunettes who'd flown in with us from New York.

'I'd never met them before. I'd say they were no older than 17, very innocent-looking.

. . .

Virginia disclosed that Mr Clinton's vice-president Al Gore and his wife, Tipper, were also guests of Epstein on his island.

. . .

'I had no clue that anything was up,' Virginia says. [They separated shortly thereafter.] 'The Gores seemed like a beautiful couple when I met them. All I knew was that Mr Gore was a friend of Jeffrey's and Ghislaine's. Jeffrey didn't ask me to give him a massage.

'There might have been a couple of other girls there on that trip but I could never have imagined this guy would do anything wrong. I was planning to vote for him when I turned 18. I thought he was awesome.'

APPENDIX N: MY EMAIL TO JULIE BROWN, 3/12/19

Ms. Brown -

Mr. Celli [one of my lawyers] has forwarded your letter to me. I am writing this letter despite my belief that it is unlikely that you could or would fairly assess the evidence of my innocence. I write this in sadness and frustration rather than in anger because up to now your reporting about me has been extremely one sided and unfair. I believe the reason for that is because your report — for which the Miami Herald is proposing you for a Pulitzer— relied extensively on the credibility of Virginia Roberts (Giuffre). Even if the evidence were to conclusively prove that Roberts made up the entire story about me for money — which the evidence shows she did— it is unlikely you would publish the facts that undercut Roberts' credibility, because it would endanger your Pulitzer.

I have already provided you overwhelming evidence of Robert's long history of perjury and lying, including her false claims of meeting Al and Tipper Gore and Bill Clinton on Epstein's island. You responded that "this was not the story" you were writing, and you never reported on her demonstrable lies. Nor did you report on her own lawyer's statement that she did not tell the truth about having sex on multiple occasions with Leslie Wexner. (If Boies believed the story about Wexner, why did he not make it public? Did he extort Wexner and did Wexner pay? That's a story worth pursuing.) You never published this and other evidence of lying that I provided you.

I offered to have you come over to my apartment and review the thousands of papers of my travel, phone and other documentary evidnce that conclusively proves that it would have been impossible for me to have been in the locations where Roberts falsely claimed she had sex with me. I also quoted Boies's statement - that I can conclusively prove he made – that after reviewing all of my travel and American Express records, he believed it was "impossible" for me to have been at the locations she claims she met me, and that he was "convinced" that his client was "wrong, simply wrong " about having had sex with me. You did not refer to these records or quote Boies's acknowledgement about his client being wrong concerning me.

As you heard in court, there are emails between Sharon Churcher and Roberts that systematically prove how I came to be falsely accused: Although it is clear from the email exchange that Roberts never had sex with me, she was urged to include my name in her book manuscript because I was "famous" and that the inclusion of my name would help her sell books. As my lawyer said, she did include my name in her manuscript but not as someone who had sex with her. As you also heard in court, I am seeking to open up all the records in the case, because I know that the records will confirm my innocence. The records will also prove that at the time she claimed she was "loaned out", Roberts told her relatives and friends the names of numerous people with whom she said she had sex. But importantly, she did not include me, because she had never met me. She never accused me of having sex with her until <u>after</u> she met her current lawyers, who – according to Robert's best friend- "pressured" her into naming me to help their case and to obtain money. Roberts told her best friend, Rebecca, that she didn't want to name me, but she felt pressured by her lawyers to do so, even though it was untrue. I have a recording of her friend.

Moreover, the records will prove that Roberts deliberately lied about her age in order to falsely claim that she was underage when she had sex with Epstein's friends. The records, including her own employment records, will show that she was well over the age of consent when she claims – falsely – that she had sex with me and with others.

You never mentioned in your reporting that Roberts has claimed to have had sex with George Mitchell, Bill Richardson, Ehud Barak, Marvin Minsky and other prominent people, despite telling Churcher that she didn't remember anyone she had sex with. It is noteworthy that Roberts has never been willing to accuse me, or have her lawyers accuse me, outside of the litigation privilege. When you interviewed her, either you did not ask her directly whether she had sex with me, or if you did, you did not publish her reply. Nor did you publish the fact that she refused to tell you on the record (or presumably even off the record) that she had sex with me. If you made a deal with her lawyers not to ask her whether she had sex with me, you are obliged to publish that fact so that your readers could judge her credibility. The way you handled your interview with Roberts raises serious questions about your journalistic ethics. You are obligated to tell your readers either that she refused to answer the question about me or that she answered it only off the record, or that you didn't ask it, because of an arrangement with her lawyers. This is crucially important because Roberts and her lawyers continue to hide behind the litigation privilege when they falsely accuse me. In the video taped interview she claims to have had sex with "academics". Did you not ask her who those academics were? You then posted a photo of me and a court document that essentially asserted that I was the academic, but you never directly said that she told you that. That is extraordinarily unprofessional journalism – putting words in her mouth through visuals that she would never say verbally. Did you ask her to name the other people she accused? If so, why didn't you name them? If not, why did you not ask her, since you knew she had named very prominent people? I suspect the reason is because if you mention the names of those people, many people would not believe she is telling the truth about George Mitchell and others like him.

To my knowledge, this is the only case in modern history and certainly since the "me too" movement began where a prominent person has been accused of having sex with someone <u>he never even met</u>. In every other case, there were relationships and disputes about such matters as consent, but in my case, I categorically state that I never met this woman and that her claims about me are overtly perjurious and criminal. No one has produced an iota of evidence that I ever met either of my accusers, because I did not.

As to Sarah Ransom, she tried to sell her story to Page Six of the New York Post, claiming she had sex tapes of Hillary and Bill Clinton, Donald Trump and Richard Branson. You can confirm this with the Post reporter to whom she sent hundreds of hallucinatory emails that we are also trying to unseal. The New York Post journalist is Maureen Callahan. I hope you will call her and ask her for the many emails Ransom sent her. Callahan told me that she and her editors found Ransom to lack credibility – that she was a liar and that she was making up the story about the sex tapes. David Boies is aware of these emails and of the Post's refusal to run a story about Ransom's false accusations. But nonetheless, he and his firm submitted a perjured affidavit by her falsely accusing me. Apparently Boies's standard of credibility for filing a sworn affidavit is lower than that of Page Six. Moreover, Ransom has falsely claimed that I was her lawyer. This is provably false. Even David Boies has acknowledged that by removing that claim from a document he later submitted. I never met Sarah Ransom, I never represented her, I never had sex with her. She is lying about me as she lied about having a sex tape of Hillary Clinton. This is the nature of my accusers that you claim to believe, and report on uncritically. As you know, I am seeking to unseal all of her emails, and if I get them, I hope that you will publish them and put them on line so your readers can judge for themselves her credibility or